Chaos

Raksha Bharadia graduated from Loreto College, Calcutta University, in Arts, with History, Political Science and Economics. Raksha has authored three books which are published by Rupa: *Me: A Handbook for Life* (2006) *Roots and Wings: A handbook for Parents* (2008) *All and Nothing* (2010), and *Ten on Ten* (2016)

She has also edited thirteen titles in the *Chicken Soup for the Indian Soul* series; has worked for the show *Lakhon Main Ek*; and has been a columnist for *Femina, Ahmedabad Mirror* and with *DNA* Ahmedabad.

Her latest foray is an online portal on couple relationships for urban India, here is the link, http://www.bonobology.com/Default.aspx

Chaos

Chaos

In Romance, Sexuality and Fidelity

RAKSHA BHARADIA

RUPA

Published by
Rupa Publications India Pvt. Ltd 2019
7/16, Ansari Road, Daryaganj
New Delhi 110002

Sales centres:
Allahabad Bengaluru Chennai
Hyderabad Jaipur Kathmandu
Kolkata Mumbai

ISBN: 978-93-5333-604-2

First impression 2019

10 9 8 7 6 5 4 3 2 1

Printed by Nutech Print Services, Faridabad

Contents

Introduction

And the kind of questions that surround lengthy relationships—what is it to live with another person for a long time? What do we expect? What do we need? What do we want? What is the relation between safety and excitement, for each of us?—are the most important of our lives.

—HANIF KUREISHI

Relationships, especially long-term ones, have fascinated me with their inherent contradictions—the allure and the grimness, the pettiness and the grandeur. It would certainly be nice to live in a fairytale world of 'all is well' but there comes a point when we must perforce face the realities permeating our important relationships. The quote with which I have begun this introduction simmered within me a long time and was finally the torque leading to an enquiry on love, marriage, sex, individuality and infidelity. For, I strongly believe, 'Marriage brings together the most serious things: sex, love, children, betrayal, boredom, frustration and property.'[*]

This book is an attempt to understand relationships. I have tried to make sense of the chaos emerging from the cohabitation of two independent selves; the confusion generated by fleeting romances and by its more rooted cousin, love.

I have delved into the seemingly irreconcilable differences between the instinctiveness of sex and the reasonableness of fidelity. This enquiry has turned yet more interesting and complex, the challenges far deeper and more layered, due to the catalytic and fundamental changes in almost every facet of our lives brought about by various factors such as growing economic and social equality for women, the waning force of tradition, swift technological changes breaking barriers imposed by long-standing systems, the increasing desire for individual identity and the unmistakable impact of urbanization. Today we live in a global village. Change is in the air; its force is inexorable. We are caught in a vortex, conscious of our strong and deep traditional roots, yet increasingly aware of au courant ideas and practices in more modernized societies.

In the writing of this book I have researched long-term relationships and their dynamics in contemporary urban India. I have read extensively, books and dissertations, journals and studies. I have met historians, sociologists, sexologists, clinical psychologists, marriage therapists, legal experts at family courts, psychoanalysts, social commentators, popular culture analysts, advertising gurus, etc. Several non-professionals have generously shared with me their personal stories (I have changed names to protect their privacy). I have talked to people of all categories—

---

*Hanif Kureishi, *In Praise of Adultery*

married, single, divorced, in live-in relationships, in monogamy, in polyamory; I have also conducted surveys and polls, and all these inputs have helped in the making of this book.

I have explored sexuality through the march of time and in diverse societies; explored the impulse to infidelity; tried to understand the difficulty, pain and anxiety of intimate relationships; delved into the restless neediness of love; and into the myths of eternal romance. Some of the questions I have tried to grapple with are:

Is monogamy natural and organic? Why is monogamy synonymous with morality? Why is weightage given to fidelity in a marriage? Why the onset of boredom in marriages? Why is a single relationship expected to assuage all needs? Why the imposition of so many rules in the most unique of relationships? To what extent is it possible to share one's life if social or economic circumstances compel one to concentrate on one's own interests?

I am not the person I was when I first thought of this work. The research for it and writing it has changed me. I understand relationships better now, and yes, I am far more patient with frailties of my life partner and my own, and have learnt to see things in a larger canvas.

I hope you enjoy reading this work as much as I have enjoyed writing it.

1

Monogamy and Desire: Long-term vs Short-term

Love another, but make not a bond of love
Fill each other's cup but drink not from one cup.
Give your hearts, but not into each other's keeping
For only the hand of Life can contain your hearts.

—KAHLIL GIBRAN, *The Prophet.*

The happily-married monkey

In January 2015, it was reported that two chimpanzees, Nikita and Jason, were to be separated after living together for twenty years. The zoo authorities wished to augment their chimpanzee population and it seemed the two were not inclined to mate, even though they seemed to be the best of mates. The zoo authorities hoped Nikita would mate with Chajju, an occupant of Kanpur zoo, and produce offsprings. An online petition was soon in circulation with the subject line: Don't force 20 years of LOVE to be TORN apart!'

In human eyes the two chimpanzees were 'already happily married'. Whilst those favouring the zoo authorities' stance wished Nikita to be given the opportunity of possible sexual intercourse with another, those signing the petition were against the break-up of a happy—even if unproductive—union.

Interestingly, the chimps' condition resembles the state of a large section of married couples in India. A survey we conducted with 300 participants revealed 14 per cent had stopped having sex altogether within the first twenty years of marriage, while 64 per cent said that sex had decreased considerably. Quite a parallel to the story of the Lucknow chimps!

Nikita and Jason continued to be together in Lucknow zoo.

You might be thinking that the chimps who feature in a lot of illustrations in this book is the sad chimp we have mentioned above. Well, you are totally mistaken. Our muse, or *sutradhar,* is in fact a much closer and wiser relative—the Bonobo.

The Bonobo

Until quite recently, bonobos were thought to be smaller versions of chimpanzees but they are actually more closely related to us.

We differ from bonobos by only 1.6 per cent in our DNA structures, and if this scientific fact does not impress you, maybe this fact will: Bonobos, like no other species but humans, hold hands while walking around, and during copulation, look deep into each other's eyes!

Martin Surbeck from the Max Planck Institute for Evolutionary Anthropology found that bonobo mothers help to usher their sons into the best spots for meeting females, and they sometimes help their sons during conflicts with other males. Imagine getting help from your mum to get laid! That's the bonobo style! But sounds familiar, doesn't it?

These 'hippies of the primate world'—as primatologist De Waal, professor at Emory University, calls them—use sex, instead of resorting to violence, as a method of social control. Intimacy makes it hard to stay angry. See the resemblance?

How did we transform from living in the jungles to living in our minds? Perhaps with our 'modern', 'cultured' system of monogamy!

What really is monogamy?

Monogamy, in its simplest understanding, is the union of one man with one woman, voluntarily entered into, to the exclusion of all others. Its boundaries—physical, economical and social—are strictly policed by laws and norms. Sexual fidelity and exclusivity is an important determinant of the specialness and trust in the relationship. Monogamy as a term does not describe sexual fidelity, but merely the act of marriage to a single person.

In our current usage, though, we blur the concepts. We have begun to perceive sexual fidelity as the ultimate expression of love and commitment. Marriage is a social and legal institution where a couple pledges to live with each other till death do them part. In this book, when I speak of monogamy, it will be strictly in the sense of being married to one person at a time.

Is monogamy natural and normal? Or are we using the term 'natural' for what is 'normal' or prevalent today?

Theorists have claimed that married, monogamous couples are the natural unit of human society. That sexual monogamy is an essential and 'natural' model of social and reproductive organization. That social monogamy facilitates a fulfilling and stable life. The question we need to ask ourselves at this point is, what exactly, is 'natural' and 'normal'?

Are we using the term 'natural' for what is 'normal' or prevalent today? Natural can be defined in many ways, but according to etymology, it essentially means having some relationship with nature. Normal is a statistical term, generally referring to a characteristic or behaviour that is possessed or demonstrated by a large percentage of a population.

Strictly speaking, if we were to live naturally, a man would want to chase anything in a skirt on his way to the office and in the office, and a woman would perhaps want to elope with her gym trainer who looked like Salman Khan, if only for a night. And if 'normal' is the average next-door-neighbour, then there are high chances that he or she is secretly having an affair, and if not, at least thinking about it.

Monogamy, with its unarguable social advantages, may be the norm in most of our contemporary modern societies but history and biology show that strict monogamy is not a one-size-fits-all. The truth of our natures is that many of us desire sex with more than one person whether we may be able to have it or not. As much as we may value fidelity, we are biologically fashioned to seek fresher sexual pastures—'new' sex arouses more potent sexual feelings than the 'old'. Familiarity may not breed contempt but it does lower a couple's copulation rates. Whether a person succeeds at being sexually monogamous depends as much on biology as environment. Monogamy is a condition imposed by society and is not a genetic disposition. Monogamy is invented for order and investment—but not necessarily because it's 'natural.'

Did you know?

Globally, in a survey of 1,231 societies, only 186 were monogamous. Among the rest, 588 had frequent polygyny, 453 had occasional polygyny, and 4 practised polyandry—when one woman is married to more than one husband at a time. (Source: *Ethnographic Atlas*). That means only about 15 per cent of societies are monogamous.

And if we just scratch the surface a little, we will see the true nature of relationships in this puny 15 per cent that is monogamous. Many, if not most, are faced with the detritus of infidelity—messy divorces, serial monogamy, and where couples do manage to stick to the norm, a dead, passionless marital bed leading to deep frustration, sometimes followed by marital squabbles, perhaps even crimes of passion.

Researching for this book I met more than a score of marriage/sex professionals across India. Most of them implicated infidelity, or the suspicion of it, as the reigning troublemaker in urban marriages today—as high as 50 per cent of the cases that came to them. And 'it is on a steep rise' said Neeru Kanwar, a marriage therapist from Delhi. She said that six out of every ten people at her doorstep, for counselling, had infidelity issues.

Delhi Family Courts observed rising cases of extramarital relationships among married couples; extramarital affairs were also the main reason for divorce by mutual consent, as listed by counsellors and lawyers. Iti Kanungo, Principal Counsellor at Patiala House Family Court, said, 'On an average, each family court receives ten to fifteen petitions for divorce because of adultery every month. The record books at the family courts are flooded with galloping infidelity statistics and the increase in adultery.'

Monogamy and marriages began when agriculture took over. Thus, on a reduced scale of 1:100, if humans were 200 years old, we started marrying only 13 years ago. The real 'tradition' was to roam free.

Mosuo Tribe: A black hole in the starlit sky of monogamy

A matrilineal society which has no monogamy or prostitution, and instead, has free sex almost as in prehistoric times!

Lugu Lake in Southwest China is home to the Mosuo. It is a remote place high in the mountains, and a rare place on this globe. For over 2,000 years, the Mosuo have been a matrilineal society. In their language there are no words for 'father' and 'husband', nor for 'prostitution'.

When a girl crosses puberty, she is given her own room in the house, a room that has a door to the street outside plus a door to the inner chambers. She is free to invite any male she wants to spend the night with, the only condition being that he has to leave the house by morning. Any child resulting from this un-wedlock, is reared by the girl's 'family', which is made up of her brothers and sisters, mother and aunts, uncles. All members in a house are related by blood, all know each other since birth. There is no concept of marriage, nor of monogamy.

All children, like our prehistoric ancestors, are—as per our modern sensibilities—bastards. Fathers go scot free, they are not expected to economically or otherwise support the children. They may meet once a year, and exchange a hug and a gift. That is, if fatherhood is at all established, for which there is no pressure.

Probably the most famous aspect of Mosuo culture is their practice of 'walking marriages' (or 'zou hun' in Chinese). Traditionally, a Mosuo woman who is interested in a particular man will invite him to come and spend the night with her in the room. Such pairings are generally conducted in the secret at night and the man will then return home early in the morning.

What if, like the Mosuo, we cherished the dignity and autonomy of those we loved? What if, in other words, sex, love, and economic security were as available to us as they were to our pre-agricultural ancestors? If fear is removed from jealousy, what's left?

Thus, monogamy is not the one and only way of life on earth.

When we believe that we have always been monogamous and that any deviation from it is unnatural and abnormal, the need to reprimand the deviants seems the right course of action!

This line by Noel Biderman, the CEO of Ashley Madison, a dating site for married people boasting of more then 30 million users worldwide, refuses to fade out, 'What made the greatest impression on me was just how vulnerable the idea of monogamy must be. Otherwise, why would anyone who just clears their throat and points out that monogamy might not be for everyone, be accused of ruining it for everyone else?'

I like my marriage, just not all of it...

2

On the Wings of Love

Dubai airport is a transglobal transit point. I saw them sauntering past, walking hand in hand, giggling and laughing. His black T-shirt had the word 'boyfriend' crossed out with bold red strokes. Beneath it was inscribed 'husband'. Her black T-shirt said 'wife' with 'girlfriend' crossed out. Then the wife whispered something in the husband's ears. He took her hands delicately to his lips and kissed them. She laughed, her pleasure evident. The husband now leaned over and murmured something in the wife's ears and she patted the nape of his neck. I watched as they exchanged a kiss on the lips.

On the backs of their T-shirts was written 'Just Married'.

'Awwww,' went my younger daughter. My elder daughter exclaimed 'Oh, so sweet!' My husband chuckled.

Before this little cameo played out, we had been slouching in our seats, bored and exhausted. After it, we all seemed invigorated. The couple was now a few paces ahead of us. My

elder daughter slipped into her shoes and tugged at me. I quickly slipped my feet into my own shoes and we both began trailing the 'Just Married' pair.

Following them, we observed the reactions of the people who noticed the two passing by. Coffee cups and liquor glasses froze mid-air, people glanced up from their reading; eyes followed the happy couple strolling past, smiles lighting up the faces of the observers. The happy 'Just Married' couple left much joy and gladness in their wake.

Love, when bathed in romance, does make the world go round. And we can't but help step in, even if for a short spin. For, if nothing else, it instantly reminds us of the magic of our own romance(s), however small or big, long or fleeting, past or current. Romantic love, even in reminiscence, has the power to own us in a snap, even if it is for a few brief moments—the hope of love, the promise of it, the knowledge of all the places it has taken us. Peaks of ecstasy, depths of intensity, throes of involvement, the pleasure of longing! We have all known such feelings—the complete owning of, or being owned by, the other; the 'I-can't-breathe-I-can't-sleep-I-love-him/her-so-much' innervation. In such moments our existential angst is rendered mute, for we know why we are here—it is for our beloved. And for then at least—whether for a few hours, days, months or years—we know that we were desired and wanted, cherished and worshipped. It is enough. Everything else can be dealt with.

Recall the popular Doris Day song, 'Everybody loves a lover'. In falling in love, you love yourself, love the world, and you feel everybody in the world loves you. We all love lovers in the thrall of romance. It's charming and heartwarming. For the lovers themselves, everything seems perfect. A state of euphoria pervades their moments. Their love knows no barriers, rationality matters not a whit. Such romantic love is untradeable, uncaring of profit or loss; cannot be predicted, cannot be banned. It is hopelessly hopeless, boundlessly devotional, totally spontaneous—and utterly, inescapably charming and enticing.

It makes us feel alive every moment!

In the letters addressed by Mariana Alcoforado,* the Portuguese nun, to her unfaithful seducer, a phrase read, 'I thank you from the bottom of my heart for the desperation you cause me and I detest the tranquility in which I lived before I knew you'.

Romantic love may be doomed to misfortune, but it is a still greater misfortune never to have known it.

The two aspects of *Shringar Ras, milan* and *viraha,* keep the heart deeply engaged and anxious. Milan is communion, uniting, togetherness. Viraha is separation, yearning and loneliness.

---

*Gabriel Joseph De Lavergne. *The Letters of a Portuguese Nun (Marianna Alcoforado*).

Joy and ache alternate in equal intensity. Yet, deep inside non-fulfilment is hidden the fragrance of intense fulfilment. The endless dance continues... we are awake in every pore.

In *The Rationality of Emotion,* de Sousa* notes that although reason is central to many human activities, emotional capacities may be of equal or greater importance in enabling one to lead the good life. Thus, loyalty and love may be more important than reason in enduring relationships.

Romantic love makes us experience eternity

'Death leaves a heartache no one can heal, love leaves a memory no one can steal.'

From an Irish headstone.
(Richard Puz, *The Carolinian*)

It gives us a sense of integrity

In love there is a coming together of mind, body and soul.

A friend, speaking of the time when she was deep in the throes of love said, 'Money, people, position did not matter to me. I was content in loving.'

In the beloved's eyes we become unique

A dialogue repeated often in hundreds of movies when the father or the mother advises a lovesick hero or heroine is: 'Forget him. I shall get you someone far better.' And the lovesick protagonist

---

*The Rationality of Emotion Ronald de Sousa.

says, 'No. Only her. No one but her!' And the audience identifies completely with this statement.

'Don't you think I was made for you?' Zelda Fitzgerald asked F. Scott Fitzgerald shortly after they met.[*] 'I feel like you ordered, and I was delivered to you.'

We are a population of five billion plus. But the person we love and the person who loves us sets us apart from these billions. Like a friend said, '*Apne pyar ke saath tum is badi duniya ke ander ek choti duniya banati ho.* (You and your beloved create your own world inside this huge world).' With our lover we become a self-contained unit. Our beloved becomes a one-point-stop for everything as our needs for others cease, even if temporarily.

Like Pritish Nandy said in an interview, 'The problem with love is that it is synonymous with life. The day you stop falling in love is the day you might as well say quits to life and go on the much spoken about *teerth* that your grandma was talking to you about.' [†]

We tell our lovers the stories of our lives—mundane and deep, silly and serious, painful and pleasant—and they become a witness to our lives. In their eyes our lives become unique. For us there is the sanguinity that perhaps our stories are worth telling...

**Dear Scott, Dearest Zelda: The Love Letters of F. Scott and Zelda Fitzgerald.* Ed. Cathy W. Barks.

†Source: https://timesofindia.indiatimes.com/life-style/spotlight/Forbidden-love-Go-grabit/articleshow/5569553.cms Created: Feb 16, 2010,

We become their priority

When we are in love, our life, in all its triviality and grandiosity, becomes as significant to the beloved as it is to us. He/she is closest to understanding and perhaps feeling our pain and happiness. Our trials become something they have to help us with, our joys expand into theirs. As Seymour Epstein said,* 'To love is to derive satisfaction from observing the welfare and fulfilment of the loved one… I know I love you because it makes me happy to see you happy'.

And, the lover fills us up. Our moments and days. Our sense of self. We feel complete. Even when the person is not there physically, we feel complete in their thoughts.

A person I interviewed said, 'It is as if an invisible presence is filling you up, making the sunset prettier, the breeze a musician and the moon your personal chandelier. The world indeed is my oyster.'

The beloved knows you like none other

And then there is also the euphoric avalanche of emotions that go along with intimately discovering another person and becoming intimately known yourself. A person I spoke to said, 'Who else will know that I prefer the bloom of the yellow flowers on the Tikoma in our society driveway to an expensive Scotch. Or that disturbing my evening walk schedule is a sure-shot way to make me see red! Who else but me will know that he is laughing

---

* John H. Harvey, Ann L. Weber. *Odyssey of the Heart: Close Relationships in the 21st Century*. Second edition.

uncontrollably because of what Claire said in *Modern Family* or that he loves his biscuits a little damp and less chewy.'

Yes, we delight in discovering that the other knows us so well, often plumbing depths within us which have hitherto been unbeknownst even to us. Perceiving our potential, lovers push us beyond self-imposed limits. Sometimes it is the beloved's faith in us that inspires us to excel beyond our own expectations.

An interviewee told me, 'He loves poetry—that's why the two of us gel. But, before I came into his life, he did not know anything about poetry. Being in the police services he did not have that space. I saw it in him, the desire for tender art. I taught him from scratch. We started with the English version of *Gitanjali*. Today he reads high-level poetry. That is what I ask myself, this has to be love.'

Unending love

I seem to have loved you in numberless forms, numberless times
In life after life, in age after age, forever.
My spellbound heart has made and remade the necklace of songs,
That you take as a gift, wear round your neck in your many forms,
In life after life, in age after age, forever.

Whenever I hear old chronicles of love, its age-old pain,
Its ancient tale of being apart or together
As I stare on and on into the past, in the end you emerge,
Clad in the light of a pole star piercing the darkness of time:
You become an image of what is remembered forever.

You and I have floated here on the stream that brings from the fount
At the heart of time, love of one for another.
We have played alongside millions of lovers, shared in the same
Shy sweetness of meeting, the same distressful tears of farewell
Old love but in shapes that renew and renew forever.

Today it is heaped at your feet, it has found its end in you
The love of all man's days both past and forever:
Universal joy, universal sorrow, universal life.
The memories of all loves merging with this one love of ours—
And the songs of every poet past and forever.

Rabindranath Tagore

And the world stops

When lovers kiss, the world pauses. Lovers find a microcosmic world of their own; others cease to exist or to matter.

'We are discontinuous beings, individuals who perish in isolation in the midst of an incomprehensible adventure, but we yearn for our lost continuity. Only the beloved can in this world bring about what our human limitations deny, a total blending of two beings, a continuity between two discontinuous creatures.'*

No wonder romantic love enchants us so. And the idea of 'happily ever after'.

---

*William Pawlett, *Georges Bataille: The Sacred and Society.*

Our fascination with love stories is evidenced in our art forms and entertainments. Romantic love exists in most cultures whether liberal or conservative, and has been there through time past and present, across all social strata and religions. Its near universality and the emphasis placed on it by society, by media (in India, by Bollywood and popular literature), keeps the fire raging in our hearts and minds, long after the sparks have died down. We are *in love* with love!

Yes, we are in love with *romantic love*! Its embers smoulder within us. All it takes is a spark to flare up again. Many of us long for that to happen. And then we come across a couple bathed in love's aura, like I did at Dubai airport. Their aura permeates the atmosphere and washes across the onlookers. Ever watched the faces of people (of any age) in a movie theatre seeing a romantic sequence? Smiles, powered from within; hearts somersaulting. It is like we, too, are flying on the wings of love!

Our own mythology is replete with stories of romantic love. One of our creation myths alludes to the romantic love-play between Shiva and Shakti—creation resulted from the game of hide-and-seek they played. Parvati desired Shiva and won him over with great difficulty. Their love transcended the limits of life and death and they are believed to be together for countless lives.

Kamadeva, the Hindu god of carnal love, has much romance interwoven into his myths. Surdas immortalized Krishna and Radha as the most enduring lovers. Shringar Ras flowered in the land of Vraj and the gopis yearned for the flute-playing Krishna. Kalidas's romantic Meghadūta transcends all time with its romance. There are countless stories of love like those of Dushyant and Shakuntala, Nala and Damyanti, et al. This deep bonding has been our ideal over centuries!

Did you know?

There is a school of thought for whom the general perception is that romance is a luxury and the prerogative of developed nations like Europe and America. And that it has percolated in our systems via the larger forces of globalization. To be in love, in thrall, to romance, is seen as a subtle example of cultural acuity—of which the general populace is inherently incapable—their paroxysms are covetous and lascivious. But according to William Jankowiak, the editor of *Romantic Passion,* out of 166 cultures that they surveyed for the universality of romantic love, they found it in 148—a whopping 89 per cent! He says, 'For many historians, romantic love never existed outside of Europe. For others it occurs in non-western nation-states among only the cultural elite, those individuals lucky enough (or unlucky if you will) to have the necessary sophistication and leisure time to cultivate an aesthetic appreciation for such a subjective experience. It has long been taken for granted that romantic love is the fruit of cultural refinements and not an experience readily available or accessible to non-westerners in general.'* His survey effectively suggests that romantic love is practically a universal phenomenon.

---

*Ed. William Jankowiak, *Romantic Passion: A Universal Experience?* (revised edition).

The need to be together

If romantic love is near-universal, so is marriage; but not together, not always in tandem. Historically, they were perceived as quite antithetical to each other till relatively recent times. Marriage was about the long haul, romantic love was intrinsically short-lived. Whilst poetry and legend may have sung paeans to romantic love, most cultures or societies imposed—particularly in the West—a terrifying penalty on it, and it was considered forbidden, sinful, and punishable in quite fearful ways. Religious and secular rulers unambiguously disconnected the passion of romantic love from marriage. Whilst there existed an inclination to sentimentalize passion and romance, they were not deemed suitable in reality for the sustenance of married life and the family, or for the administration and progress of the state, society and religion.

Today, we increasingly consider romantic love as a precursor to sexual congress, and to marriage.

The advent of marriage

Marriage developed independently in civilizations. Early Sumerian marriage agreements which date to the third millennium BC are amongst the oldest records relating to marriage. Many systems of marriage existed—polygamy, polyandry, group marriage, monogamy, multi-partner, etc. For thousands of years marriage has been used as a tool for survival and to organize people's place in the economic, social and political spheres. It was also the primary way of organizing work along lines of age, gender and specialization.

The primary functions of marriage, apart from the sexual,

revolved around meeting basic needs like food production, shelter, and physical safety. And it had huge economic trade-offs. Until the late-eighteenth century, historian Margaret Hunt* points out, marriage was 'the main means of transferring property, occupational status, personal contacts, money, tools, livestock and women across generations and kin groups.'

For most men, the dowry that a wife brought was the biggest infusion of cash, goods, or land that they would ever acquire. For most women, finding a husband was the most important investment they could make in their economic future. For the rich and the propertied classes, marriage was an arrangement between two families to cement ties and merge assets. The commoners used marriage as a way of arranging plots of land, which were doled out in random strips. It was a tool to expand and strengthen one's circle of people to rely upon in times of famine and violence. Marriage, more often than not, resulted in beneficial alliances. Traders and artisans of the same craft often married into each other's circle to share supplies.

Procreation, child-rearing, and mutual helpfulness were the widely-held social functions that marriages fulfilled. It allowed the framework for sexual gratification in a safe, non-conflict environment.

And then there were the political functions—marriages made to facilitate peace treaties, for strengthening territories, gaining alliances, exerting influences. The ancient world observed marriage as a means of preserving power, where rulers married off their daughters to foreign alliances to acquire lands or preserve their own.

---

*Gloria L. Main, *Peoples of A Spacious Land.*

The ancient religions of India sanctified matrimony. One was considered incomplete and unholy if one did not marry—except for those who chose to become sanyasis. The marriage of two individuals was considered to be not just for one lifetime, but for seven or more lives. Without a wife a man could not progress to the grihasth ashram (the life-stage of a householder). Without marriage there could be no offspring. Without a son there could be no release from the cycle of reincarnation, no attainment of moksha. Given the sanctity of marriage, its annulment was not an option.

'In Gujarat there is a proverb, a song that goes, '*Kahin ucha, kahin nicha*'. It's called 'kajoda', which means some mismatch. Like a husband could be very tall and the wife very short. You could see kajoda in a lot of ways. And those marriages worked too. If there was a kind of synchrony between the bride and groom, it was good, but if not, kajodas worked too.' Doctor Gaurang Jani, professor of Sociology at Gujarat University, said to me while reflecting on the current trend of love marriages today and the ideology of compatibility. 'Marriage had different drivers, not the ones we have today.'

For all socioeconomic groups, marriage was the most important marker of adulthood and respectability.

NIMHANS Professor of Clinical Psychology, Dr Ahalya Raguram, said to me during an interview, 'From our cultural perspective, people getting married is a social expectation. In some ways people see it as "normalcy". And so people who don't marry are in some ways perceived to be failures. In the West, the ability to have a date, especially on weekends, and the ability of being able to find a partner for a date, is seen as a part of social success. The ability to get married and have a family is seen as a measure of success in life here in our culture.'

In short, marriage was bread and butter, shelter and commitment, children's lives, and a whole network of family members of both partners.

In the well-received film *Saaransh*, at the heart of the story was the abiding relationship—the love story—of an old couple living in Mumbai, who had been married to each other a long time.

'How come,' the wife asks her elderly husband at one point, 'How come, in all these years, you have never once told me that you love me? Look at this young couple, they are professing love for each other all the time. And look at us. No love, nor any romance. Why are we married? Tell me. I really want to know.'

The old man racks his brains but can't find an appropriate, truthful answer. Clearly, for the first time in his forty years of married life, he is caught in the chaos of romance!

Almost all married couples have sometime in the past, or will in the future, be in the same unenviable position as this old man in the film. The partner who we sleep with, eat with, play house with, might one day, all of a sudden, point a gun at us and say, 'Hands up! Tell me, do you really love me? Be honest.'

What is it about romance that rattled the solid foundation of marriage of this sixty-year-old woman?

Where does romance fit in?

Today we believe that romantic love should be the foundation on the basis of which two people lay down the blueprints of a lifetime of togetherness. All else will or should fall in place. Our ancestors did not have it this simple. While marriage has existed as a central element of life in nearly every global culture in recorded history, in none of them, till very recently, have we married for love, especially romantic love. For thousands of years, marriage as an institution had done well, not *because* of love but *despite* it. Love was always considered a weak and a poor reason for marriage.

'In 1800, the idea of marrying for love was ludicrous,' said Eli Finkel, lead author in a study on marriage, and professor of Psychology at Northwestern University. 'That isn't to say that people didn't want love from their marriage; it just wasn't the point of marriage.'

It was desirable for love, or at least affection, to develop after marriage. But love was not the main thing that people took into account in deciding when and whom to marry. It did not factor into the decision-making. A courtesan or concubine filled the role of emotional and sexual partner. In the twelfth and thirteenth centuries, European aristocracy viewed extramarital affairs as the highest form of romance, untainted by the gritty realities of daily life; where the daily grind existed, love could not! In ancient India, falling in love before marriage was considered a disruptive, antisocial act. In some Chinese dialects, a term for love didn't traditionally apply to feelings between husband and wife—it was used to describe an illicit, socially disapproved relationship. Both the ancient Greeks and medieval Europeans thought lovesickness was a type of insanity, and that it was almost indecent to love a spouse too ardently!

In fact, love and marriage were once widely regarded as

incompatible with one another for all practical reasons. Marriage demanded calm heads on two shoulders working in unison—even with differing agendas and priorities—day after day, and year after year. Romantic love needed intense emotional involvement, demanding quite different priorities of the two involved—and such love was, by its very nature, transient, likely to fade with time. The certainty and security that a marriage demanded was antithetical to the mystery and adventure that romantic love thrived on. Where marriage demanded logic, rationality and arrangement, romantic and passionate love lived on anarchy, arbitrariness and chaos. While marriage demanded commitment and obligations, passionate love considered anything not arising out of its own centre, as less worthy. While marriage sought safety and stability, passionate love sought neither, thriving on the intensity of longing.

Love is in the air

The ideal of love as a primary reason for marriage began to spread in the late-eighteenth and early-nineteenth century; the shift became clear during the Romantic Movement, and in the Victorian era, the expectation of romance became the dominant way of conceiving love and marriage.

As Enlightenment thinkers pioneered the idea that life was about the pursuit of happiness and people took more control of their love lives, they began to demand the right to end unhappy unions. As Lawrence Stone puts it, 'It was not…until the Romantic movement and the rise of the novel, especially the pulp novel, in the nineteenth century, that society at large accepted a new idea—that it was normal and indeed praiseworthy for young men and women to fall passionately in love, and that there must be something wrong with those who have failed to have such an overwhelming experience sometime in late adolescence or early manhood [sic].'*

Suddenly, couples were expected to invest more of their emotional energy in each other and eventually, in their children, rather than in their natal families, their kin, their friends, and their patrons. Marriage had become primarily a personal contract between two equals seeking love, stability and happiness. In other words, marriage had become 'personal'.

The ideals of marriage shifted from a tool for survival and protection of property to one that had personal fulfilment and happiness as its central goals. In the past, marriage was sacred, and love—if it existed at all—was a consequence of marriage. Now love was sacred, and marriage, secondary.

While the medieval and early modern models assumed a fundamental incompatibility between marriage and romance, we now assume their inseparability. Marriage is still popular and predominant as the primary way of propagating families, but its meaning has shifted. Once a binding contract which fixed one's position within the social structure, it has become an optional and soluble sign of commitment to someone with whom one has fallen in love.

Doctor Gaurang Jani traces the stirrings of romance in the Indian marriage system to social reformers. He says, 'As they propagated the ideals of equality, freedom and choice, it trickled

---

*Passionate Attachments: Thinking about love; Eds Willard Gaylin and Ethel Person.

down to the sphere of marriages too. Inspired by the modern Western ideals of individualism and personal happiness, the youth began to think of mate selection as a matter of personal choice, rather than the prerogative of parents or guardians. Agreeableness—rather than the otherwise accepted parameters based on economics, caste, endogamy, etc.—became the new benchmark. Literature, theatre and mostly cinema with its projection of romance and romantic songs, pushed the idea of romance further into the urban Indian household. The silver screen was dominated by the kings of romance'.

'Till as recently as thirty or forty years back, we did not have "kitchen romance" in our homes. The kitchen in the joint-family system was the exclusive domain of womenfolk. But with nuclear families, all that changed drastically. Today, most of the kitchen appliances are sold projecting kitchen romances. The demographic shift from joint to a nuclear family system has made romance in marriage a continuing idea. Romance is a sellable commodity.'

Think of the famous tag line that sums this up: *Jo apni biwi se kare pyar woh Prestige se kaise kare inkar!*

Rapid globalization, jobs facilitating increased mingling of men and women, marriage legislations, etc. have further led to the rise of love marriages in urban India. Greater proportion of women than ever before are part of the workforce now, including the service sectors. With greater prosperity, the aspiration and desires of the populace has changed. Exposure to Western cultural influences through mass media is often greatest in urban environments, seeping eventually into other strata of our society. And this exposure weakens the traditional norms of arranged marriages.

Dr Dorothy who works at NIMHANS, Bengaluru, and specializes in couples' counselling, cites migration and immigration to be the two big factors that have influenced the way we look at romance and marriage. 'We have a lot of people from the West in Bengaluru because of IT jobs. The foreigners with their lifestyles and value systems deeply influence the emerging youth mindsets, especially of those working with or under them. I find the biggest change in the ideology from a socialistic view of life to an individualistic view.'

Another major change is the contemporary mother-daughter relationship. 'Mothers of today wants to give daughters every opportunity and vantage point that so far was the exclusive privilege of the male child—education, liberty in clothing, mobility, freedom to chalk out career choices, etc. It is no surprise that these girls are willing to pick their own life partners based on the people they meet at workspace and otherwise,' says Jani.

Love-cum-arranged marriage

A new trend has emerged in India where though the youth select their life partners themselves, it is done with parental approval. Or the parents select the prospective spouse based on their children's approval. Parents and elders try and ensure the boy or girl (as the case may be) is from a similar social and economic status so that the potential for post-marriage conflict is minimized.

Prospective brides and grooms have found new ways to negotiate traditional customs and manoeuvre them, while at the same time, retaining the historical and sacred heritage.

While young adults in India do not wish their parents to select their spouses for them, the cultural environment and societal norms do not support Western-style dating either. This is especially true of non-metros. In this scenario, selecting a spouse with the involvement of parents serves as a convenient middle ground. Under this system, unlike in American style dating, prescreened young men and women are permitted a brief period of courtship during which they can decide if they want to get married to each other. Thus, the traditional system of arranged marriage is modified so that children can exercise some autonomy in the spouse selection process, and parents can continue to exercise some control over the choice of their children's spouse.

The big, fat, happy monogamous marriage!

Marriage has become the ultimate expression of love today.

At last, romance, sex and intimacy have all come together to nest exclusively under this 'perfect canopy' of the modern monogamous marriage. Men and women choose their marital partners based on 'chemistry' or at least some version of compatibility and agreeableness. The word 'soulmate', that we are all obsessed with, is about meeting *the* special one meant for each of us. Even in arranged marriages, boys and girls spend sufficient time testing the heart-connect before they give a willing nod to their parents.

We have honeymoons to celebrate the romance in marriage,

and we have a host of special anniversaries—first time they saw each other to the first time they felt the stirrings of love, from the first tête-à-tête to the date he proposed, from wedding anniversary to the day they cooked their first meal together, etc. etc. At every little or significant turning, the romance inherent in it is brought out, reminisced over and revalidated.

Romantic love as a basis for two people coming together, and staying together, is a dealmaker; its absence can very well turn into a deal-breaker! Many marriages end up in naught if the couples fail to find the magic of love in each other's arms. The legal acceptability of no-fault divorce, or the ones filed under the term 'incompatibility', stress on the omnipotent role of romantic love in marriages today. The decree is unambiguous and emphatic—don't underestimate the heart anymore!

'Happily ever after' now seems very achievable. Modern marriage skillfully harmonizes the needs of the heart, the body and the herd—a happy cementing of an emotional coupling with the socially desirable and state-approved one.

Many of us will identify saying something on these lines at our wedding:

I have found everything in you.

I will love you *like this* forever. I shall never desire anyone again.

I am yours, every bit of me, as you are mine forever.

Yet the reality as we know is different. Fast forward some years and the lines change completely!

G. B Shaw, in his book *Getting Married,* said, 'But the actual result is that when two people are under the influence of the most violent, most insane, most delusive, and most transient of passions, they are required to swear that they will remain in that excited, abnormal, and exhausting condition continuously until death do them part.'

The chaos of romance

'The one obstacle love can't overcome is time,' Denis de Rougemont says acerbically in *Love in the Western World*.

We have all known the ecstasy and the angst of romance. We have lived years in moments and felt the ocean within us, when in its thrall. But before we know it, our Prince Charming turns into a frog. The lovely woman turns into Surpanakha! The honeymoon is over, as it must inevitably.

Once a wise American taxi driver taking us to Vegas told me, 'I think romance is the pull that brings two people together but it is not what can make them stay together.'

There is no rocket science involved in observing that, with its symptomatic obsession and idealization of the lover, romantic love is transitory in nature and not fated to last beyond a limited time span; depending on individual proclivities it may vanish within days, persevere for weeks or months, or linger at best for a couple of years.

Albert Einstein said, 'How on earth are you ever going to explain in terms of chemistry and physics so important a biological phenomenon as first love?' It seems his rhetorical question has been answered by modern scientists. Numerous scientific studies have scanned and mapped the brains of people deeply in romantic love.

According to scientists, evolution has preprogrammed us

to feel love; our bodies are suffused with a complex and heady cocktail of neurochemicals, giving the adage 'love-struck' a literal reality! Norephinephrine, or the stress hormone, shoots up our blood pressure and heart rates, making us anxious, uncertain about the response of our loved one. Dopamine, or the 'pleasure chemical', controls the 'pleasure systems' of the brain, rewarding us with enjoyment, pleasure addiction and euphoria. Adrenalin rush makes us stay up all night, and the drop in serotonin makes us obsess over our loved ones. We feel optimistic, gregarious, and on the edge; basically, we are then most likely to behave irrationally. Romantic love, a result of all these chemicals coursing through us, overwhelms our actions, attention spans and impulses.

'With time, however, the brain can no longer tolerate this continually revved-up state. The nerve endings become either immune or exhausted, and exhilaration wanes,' says Dr Michael R. Liebowitz, a Columbia University psychiatrist. The brain can no longer tolerate the onslaught of these chemicals. As he sums it up, 'If you want a situation where you and your long-term partner can still get very excited about each other, you will have to work on it, because in some ways you are bucking a biological tide.' (*Anatomy of Love*)

So the passion and euphoria of being 'love-struck' eventually subsides. If the romance goes well, the once heart-stopping messages become mundane exchanges of, 'We have to visit the class teacher', the shy locking of glances becomes a distant memory as you sit across the table to eat, and the sweet anticipation tinged with uncertainty of a phone call turns into 'Did you switch off the geyser before leaving?'

Such then, is life.

We can only feel that much before our senses become dead. Emotional aridity appears universally when we are too tired to sustain intensity any longer. The early stage of a relationship, most marked by intense attraction and infatuation, is in many ways akin to cocaine intoxication, observes Christine Meinecke, a clinical psychologist in Des Moines, Iowa. It is orchestrated, in part, by the neurochemicals associated with intense pleasure. Like a cocaine high, it is not sustainable. But for the duration—and experts give it nine months to four years—infatuation has an overwhelming effect.

Dr Dorothy, an American psychologist, measured the duration of this limerence from the moment infatuation kicked in, to the time when a 'feeling of neutrality' for the beloved set in. The most frequently witnessed time span, as well as the average, was approximately eighteen months to three years.

I asked about the fate of romance, especially of love marriages to Dr Kalpana Khatwani, a clinical psychologist who has been practising for nearly a decade. According to her experience, 'Falling in love is a chemical process…but it can't last forever. Perhaps seven to eight years at the most,' she says, 'till a family has been started and the little ones have been nicely taken care of. Then hormones drop. It is an evolutionary trick. If you do the math it falls in place well. If you have children within two years of marriage, then they would be about five when the hormones begin to slowly drop. The child has been taken care of by both the parents through the most vulnerable years. Falling in love and staying there works from an evolutionary perspective. But the process runs itself out!'

'Once the hormones drop, the real person comes out and you do not want to be joined to the hip anymore. The seven-year itch. Each one then starts finding his own role in this equation. Most women usually go towards child-rearing, going back to girls bonding with other girls; men go out—make money, focus on career, etc. Before you know it there is too much space between the two of them—that's when they come to us. The woman says her husband is very busy with his work. And the husband says the wife is always busy with the kids.'

When I asked Dr Rajan Bhonsle, Honorary Professor and Head of the Department of Sexual Medicine at K.E.M. Hospital and Seth G.S. Medical College Mumbai, about love marriages going sour, he had a completely different point to make. He said, 'Why don't we analyse the nature of these so-called love marriages? What if it is a simple infatuation that got conveniently coined as love? An attraction to any one aspect of the other—she is pretty, he is in a powerful post, she is smart, he is attentive etc. etc. And the two "fall in love" and tie the knot. They call it love, because technically, it is not arranged by parents. But is attraction really love? There are people who actually live-in for three to four years and then decide to get married. They live with the real side of each other. To me that is a more correct definition of love marriage.'

The face-off!

The thrill of pursuit is over. We have what we had been chasing. Most of the firsts of romance are over—the first skip of the heartbeat, the first exchange of secret glances, the first holding of hands, the first declaration of love, the first kiss, the first lovemaking!

Now we have unfettered access to the other, both emotional and physical, our desires have been satiated, and since we have vowed commitment to each other, we are certain of the access in future too. The charm of opening our intimate space to the other, the privilege of being in another's intimate space, has lost its novelty. We are no longer dying to know his favourite dish or song, no longer apprehensive about her likes and dislikes, or curious about what hurt her in the past or whom he was closest to. Our beloved reciprocates our un-frenzied state. The edge has waned, and with it, the anxiety and uncertainty and the chemical rush of being on that edge. We may call it maturity—or finding comfort and peace with each other—but in a very real sense we feel blasé about it. Besides, falling in love had meant merging, and now that merging has run its course.

Sometimes, the 'unmerging' that follows falling *out* of love, is ego-shattering and often traumatic.

But addicted to the stupor, to the charming state of feeling alive from our very core, we long for the feeling and unwittingly blame either the other or ourselves for the fizzed-out romance. What we had overlooked in the romance stage now bothers us; the very qualities that had appealed to us may now turn into irritants; what we had seen as the other's simplicity may now seem boring; what we had earlier perceived as perfectionism may now seem nagging; the extrovert now seems aggressive; the quiet listener, closed and aloof. Exasperated, we ask, 'Are you really the person I fell in love with?'

Just as they were not Prince Charming to begin with, they do not really turn into frogs when the chemical cocktail's effects subside.

Romantic love is notoriously precarious—obsessive, erratic, consuming, fleeting, exhilarating, depressing. Once requited, it can slip easily into boredom. It craves security and possession of the beloved, yet when this very craving finds fulfilment, the situation may seem stifling with time!

In all other relationships (where romantic love is not at play) emotions and intensity are allowed to wax and wane, and though never comfortable or pleasant for the one at the receiving end, is accepted without much fuss and chaos. But in romantic love these phases are taken as aberrations, and appear as chaos.

A friend wrote, 'Why does (love) have to be irrational and like a drug-induced high... all grand and emphasized through every action and thought... why can't it be allowed to be a little passive... allowed to wane a bit at times... why can't you just like someone you love sometimes without wanting to get into their heads … without expecting them to fire you up every time without fail.'

Attraction between couples typically wanes after two years, yet television, movies and magazines actively encourage the notion that fading romance and boredom is a sign of a failed relationship. Mass media brainwashes us with unrealistic portrayals of romantic love contributing to the construction of impossible expectations. Glorification of romance as never-ending, glamorous and fulfilling, is repeatedly reinforced via innumerable mediums. Many industries and businesses depend on it—the fashion industry, health and wellness, television shows, music, literature and of course Bollywood! A ubiquitous feature of Bollywood cinema is happy endings—concluding a film with the union of a romantic couple. Besides, they oversimplify the process of falling in love and revalidate its eternal ideal forcing us to think that it could and should be achieved. Deepak Kashyap, counselling psychologist and a certified life-skills trainer with a private practice in Mumbai said to me during an interview, 'What ruins romance is when you try to convert it into a three-hour Bollywood movie. Any book, any movie, any webcast is time-bound, and real life is long and boring. When you pack a life of three decades into a three-hour movie, you are expecting something different. And when your expectations are not fulfilled, you either attack yourself, others, or life.'

Social media—Facebook, Twitter, WhatsApp, Instagram, etc.—with their ubiquitous posts and exchanges have massively propagated the myth of romantic love. What does not get posted are the affairs, the ugly fights, the dinners without having exchanged any words, and other deeper and everyday issues. I have always felt that what we see on social media is mostly half-truths.

Dr Rajan Bhonsle says, 'So-called happy marriages are not really that happy. They look good on FB. They appear happy in parties and you think they are happy. I stay in an elite area, Cuff Parade in Mumbai. Most of the couples in my area have come to me, socially, as neighbours or with their issues. On the outside they appear great but all of them have serious issues. Well, we hide it because everyone need not know. Just like when you have an illness you do not go about telling it to others but consult a doctor. So they come to me. For a long time I would think, "They seemed so good together". I see a totally different side. But to others they still seem perfect. I always tell my clients "Don't be fooled by others projections of their perfect married life. Everyone has issues, they are just good at hiding them!"'

Another therapist, Salony Priya, based in Kolkata, specializing in marital therapy said, 'I can say with some amount of experience that the happy-in-front-of-others couples form the majority in our society. On the face you will not suspect a thing. They go to clubs, parties, lunches and dinners, host beautiful evenings, and have impeccable manners with the guests and each other. You would say, "What a nice happy couple." But in reality their husband-and-wife relationship has been over for years. Many even sleep in separate bedrooms.'

Yet there is real mettle to the relationship that has survived decades. It is in the small and big compromises that the couple makes day in and day out. It is in the letting go and holding on. It is in standing strong when the other is enfeebled—and often switching places. And certainly, there is no cause for public display of marital issues! It is our own foolishness that we get swayed by the images people generally project.

All you need is love

What do we really mean when we refer to love? Is it the running around trees and flirting seen in cinematic hits of the golden romantic age of Bollywood? Or is it the scripted attribution to fate that the lovers unite? Are soulmates destined to end up with each other? Is it that easy? However much we may negate it, consciously and subconsciously, many of our ideals and expectations of love come from cinema, songs and books. But the very basis of those is exaggeration. For scriptwriters, lyricists and popular authors, romance is love! They do not look past the courtship stage—a period when differences are easily overlooked. Yet our notions of couple relationship is subconsciously and consciously based on these.

Perhaps here, when we say love, what we mean is the craziness of new romance, because truly at one point it was *all* that one needed!

Is love enough to avoid the minor irritants of everyday life?

When you are stuck in office yet again and your spouse is waiting at home, yet again? When she is tired of the undone toothpaste cap?

Is love enough to make up for the differences in personality?

What when one is a lark and the other an owl? Or one has grown up in a big family with a natural tolerance for noise while the other has a very low threshold for it? Or one wants children, and the other doesn't? The examples are too numerous and we all have faced a few.

Is love enough to avoid conflicts?

What when an argument brews and one deals with it by clamming up while the other is like the Brahmaputra—prodigious! She doesn't like his friends, he doesn't like hers! He doesn't like her parents, she cannot stand his!

Is love enough to overcome ideological differences? Or the gender-culture lag?

What if one believes in consumerism while the other is an avowed socialist? What when one believes in space and the other in total fusion?

Dr Kushal Jain speaks of the conflict in the role expectations, where a husband has had a mother in a subservient role, putting the family first, all loving and giving towards her children and husband. Now the son has an urban, educated, and working wife. She demands more, refuses to fit in the husband's image of what a wife is. 'Even though the two love each other, there is a cultural and a gender lag. First you have to be aware of it before you can even think of ways to resolve it. And for that, one needs openness,' said Dr Jain. 'Openness is an indicator of how smart you are. Because then you can assimilate conflicting views much easily.'

Is love enough to bridge the sexual gap?

I remember the scene from the Woody Allen movie *Annie Hall*. Annie Hall (Diane Keaton) is talking to a therapist about their sex life. When the therapist asks how often they have sex, Alvy (Woody Allen) answers, 'Hardly ever. Maybe three times a week.' Annie, however, answers this way, 'Constantly. I'd say three times a week'. What better example of the difference our gender creates in respect of sexual desire!

Is love enough to heal all wounds? And enough to make you whole when you feel broken?

Is love enough to prevent future wounding? Affairs? Other betrayals? Indifference? Violence, even when verbal?

Think about it...

'All you need is love' leaves you planless and powerless to deal with all the inevitable problems of living together. Loving has two phases—loving the person because of who he/she is and loving the person despite who he/she is.

Love is a balancing act

Bipasha Roy, married for twenty years, has an interesting equation. According to her, 'Marriages should never be 50-50. That is impractical. I am a human being; today I am upset because something might have happened at work. I go home, I need my peace. That day at home, I need an understanding husband. He understands, he is also unhappy about an issue, but when I go shouting about something, I am 70—he becomes 30. Maybe he answers back one time and then keeps quiet, waiting for me to cool down. Tonight it is 70-30. Tomorrow, when he becomes 70, I become 30. Maybe I tell him sorry that I overreacted, then he tells me he shouldn't have reacted that way in front of the children. We balance it out. So, it is a question of adjustment. To last, it should always be 70-30, 30-70 or 80-20, 20-80. It can never be 50-50.'

Do opposites attract?

Opposites frequently attract but they don't stay together very long except in mass media mythology. When romantic partners share similar values, ideologies and viewpoints on the fundamentals, it becomes easier to understand, accept and respect each other. When they don't, it's hard for them to respect where the other one is spending time, money or energy. A couple I interviewed, who met while setting up a design firm and married after a ten-year courtship, went through an extremely trying time when the wife was detected with a rare disease sometime during their fourth year into marriage. He said, 'Since the two of us have built the company from scratch and we are essentially in a creative field, we not only share this burning passion but also understand our queer working moods. Our company, which is like our baby, has played the role of an entire family that kind of helps keep the couple together! Even during worst fights we had to keep the communication open because a client needed our inputs together; during other conflicts we were forced to work as a team because we could fill in different requirements that we each specialized in. At other times we just understood that the other was going through a creative block and had to be eased'. After almost a near divorce, he attributes the marriage, working primarily because they connected at many levels that had nothing to do with romance or love!

People tend to grow weary of each other's company unless they have cultivated similar values and interests. Although short-term flings with people who are very different can be quite exciting and some differences can be enriching and stimulating, long-term relationships flourish when similarity rather than dissimilarity prevails.

Love does not consist of gazing at each other but in looking outward together in the same direction.

I interviewed Professor Ahalya Raguram from NIMHANS who has been extensively involved in couples' counselling for more than three decades in the city of Bengaluru. Most of her clients are educated and come from the middle and upper strata of this thriving IT city. According to her, one of the most common issues between a couple, even as recently married as three months, is one where the two come from a completely different system of values and upbringing. 'I often wonder whether these readily-falling-in-love couples actually confuse sexual desire and the burst of attraction as love. They rush into relationships and marriage and find themselves at a counsellor's door within the first or second year of marriage. When I dig into their background, I find an eerie similarity amidst this huge corporate flock. Many of them actually have come from smaller towns. Their migration has two underlying causes—higher education, or jobs, especially in the IT sector.

Now this shift that apparently seems harmless, actually causes deep-seated inner instability. For them, the metro culture is exciting but equally uprooting too—the value systems and equations that exist in their own families and communities in a smaller town are very different from the metro lifestyle. Besides, they suddenly have this new-found freedom with the thrill of economic independence. They are on their own, earning more than they had imagined, and away from parental supervision or control. This sense of liberty shows not only in their spending habits but also percolates into their relationships. Since they work in close proximity with other young people of the opposite gender in freer and more liberated settings, they indulge in premarital sexual relationships and experimentation. In the West, this is a lifestyle. The moment one finishes school, they get into dating relationships; for them it is a measure of social abilities and success. But here, in India, this is not the case. Here youngsters in relationships, especially sexual, feel obliged to back it up with marriage, because that is what their traditional environment has taught them. Without thinking of what actually drew them to the relationship they feel they *must* get married. To many I ask, "Was it just a sexual attraction?" And their eyes broaden as if they just connected the dots. These so-called lovers have not given any thought to each other's ideologies or value systems; I can even go as far as to say that they really do not know each other at all. They actually marry for all the wrong reasons, the rush of desire many a times cloaked as romantic love.

'Besides, before actually marrying, their time with each other is spent in coffee houses. I find it funny. All the major decisions of their lives are made sitting in the coffee shops—they have their fights there, decide to break up there and make up again because it is Valentine's Day with a gift or a card and a cake! They do not think how marriage will change their relationship or what kind of roles they will need to take on. In our culture, even if it is a relationship where partners choose their own spouses, each one still comes with the family; the family can never be out of the picture. It's not that everything needs to be the same but they definitely need to figure out how they are different and how they will work out these differences. Will they be able to accommodate these differences? My experience says that these very fundamental differences in their ideologies, value systems, and family make-up, snowball into huge irresolvable issues later!'

In the book *Normal Chaos of Love*, Beck * quotes a German study on bicultural marriages which traces the developmental patterns using empirical data.

'In the period of initial infatuation an effusive optimism prevails, a feeling of blissful openness, and ... a certain pride in one's non-conformism. After going through internal and external strains there is often a phase of retreat and renewed identification with one's own background ... People discover how firmly their own value systems are anchored, often for the first time. Without this confrontation their own value systems usually remain

---

*The Normal Chaos of Love; Ulrich Beck, Elisabeth Beck-Gernsheim; Translated by Mark Ritter and Jane Wiebel

inconspicuous, unconscious—and for that reason appear to be very normal.'

Kalpana Khatwani says, 'There are many hats every human being has to wear. We need to learn to agree to disagree. If the man says that today must be a boys' night, he is right because he believes in that. And if the woman feels that my husband must be sitting home next to me because I am nursing the baby, she too is right. If both are right, then who is wrong?'

Anwar Alam, a social science professor from Jamia Millia, said, 'What if, instead of "All you need is love", we think of a basic question: What are the minimum things a man or woman needs in life, from love, from the world? What if they set the minimum criteria?'

What if we take romance as the torque of a long meaningful relationship rather than its be all and end all? What if love was a means and not an end?

To love is first of all to subtract a person from the human community, to depopulate the world, and to ignore everything that is not of the beloved. The chosen one has to prove every day that the lover was right to put him/her on this pedestal and not another.

Think of how you behave/stay/work around your mother or other everyday members or close friends in the comfort of your house or in that zone of familiarity. You are *you*, the pleasant with the unpleasant, the sweet with the sour, the charming with the annoying, etc. You are a package, a realistic one, as are the others. Now, imagine the dinner you have been dying to get an invitation to. The one that your crush will be in. And you do! Suddenly the 'I-don't-care' attitude is replaced with fixing everything that is less than perfect. You change a dozen times, work on your hair, your skin, even your attitude. You polish and you refine, you control and you restrain, you rehearse dialogues in your head, even brush up on topical matters to be more informed, and you put your best foot forward as you enter that party. Your crush does that too! Cupid strikes and the two of you hit it off.

There are the two of you putting your best faces forward and then there is Cupid, making you see nothing else but the best in the other. And the stages of love that Stendhal talks about begins; from admiration of the 'other', you go to hope (what would it be like to have the beloved in my arms) and then to love, as the beloved returns the feelings of passion. For, what is more charming than to enjoy the pleasures of love, of seeing, sharing, touching, and to be loved in return! You credit a thousand imagined perfections to your beloved as he/she does to you. As Stendhal pithily said in *On Love,* 'One need only dream up perfections to find them in the beloved.'

What about the whole package that you are? The other side? The mismatched, annoying, weak and mean part? For a while, it doesn't exist. Or perhaps you don't notice, or they fade into irrelevance!

Did you know?

Stendhal's concept of 'crystallization' is outlined in his work *On Love*. The term 'crystallization' was inspired by his 1818 journey to the Hallein salt mines, near Salzburg, where he witnessed salt crystallization with his friend Madame Gherardi. *'In the salt mines, nearing the end of the winter season, the miners will throw a leafless wintry bough into one of the abandoned workings. Two or three months later, through the effects of the waters saturated with salt which soak the bough and then let it dry as they recede, the miners find it covered with a shining deposit of crystals. The tiniest twigs no bigger than a tom-tit's claw are encrusted with an infinity of little crystals scintillating and dazzling. The original little bough is no longer recognizable; it has become a child's plaything, very pretty to see. When the sun is shining and the air is perfectly dry the miners of Hallein seize the opportunity of offering these diamond-studded boughs to travellers preparing to go down to the mine.'*

However, it was not the salt's crystallization alone that inspired Stendhal's thoughts. During one of their visits to the salt mines, both he and Madame Gherardi were introduced to a Bavarian officer who joined their company. What Stendhal witnessed between his friend and this officer was to become the basis for his theory. The officer began to 'fall in love' with Madame Gherardi, visible to Stendhal; but what was surprising to Stendhal was his compliments of her hand, which had been scarred by bout of smallpox in her childhood. The officer saw in Madame Gherardi the perfection that Stendhal was blind to. In this moment of realization, Stendhal noticed Madame Gherardi playing with a salt crystal-covered branch, the sunlight causing them to glitter like diamonds, and from this, his concept of mental 'crystallization' was born. He explained his thoughts later to his friend, Madame Gherardi:

> *The effect produced on this young man by the nobility of your Italian features and those eyes of which he has never seen the like of, is precisely similar to the effect of crystallization upon that little branch of hornbeam you hold in your hand and*

which you think so pretty. Stripped of its leaves by the winter it was certainly anything but dazzling until the crystallization of the salt covered its black twigs with such a multitude of shining diamonds that only here and there can one still see the twigs as they really are.

And in their defence, we can say that they believe in this perfection with all their strength. She is not delusional when she tells him he is the most desirable, sensual man on the planet, even if all her friends think he is quite dull. He is not lying when he tells her she is brilliant and beautiful, even if no one else agrees.

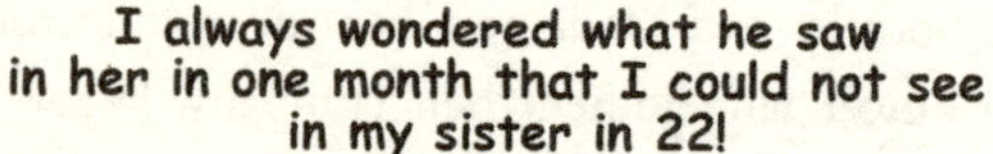

What kind of knowing is involved when we speak of our beloved when in throes of this crystallization phase? Is what we think is love based on reality or fantasy?

'You have changed', is something we have often accused our beloved of, or have been charged with by them.

When the intensity of love wanes, we stop idealizing and begin to see things we don't like in our lovers. It's not so much that we don't like who they really are, it's just that it had seemed, in love's illusion, that they were everything we really liked. And so while we fight about sex, housekeeping, money, how many drinks per party or how many stag nights a month, we are actually negotiating the nitty-gritty of living together with the 'real' person that we actually meet every single day once the crystallization wears off.

Arunava Sinha, translator of contemporary, modern and classic Bengali fiction into English, made an interesting point to me during an interview. He said, 'Most of the love or arranged marriages take place in the early 20s or early 30s but you don't even know much about yourself then. You are changing, your understanding of the world is changing. Somewhere around 35 or 40, we get some semblance of who I am and what I want and we wake up to "this is not who I want". The real choices or understanding of love and marriage actually do not happen till the early 40s. And in our country the structure is such that you don't think of what will make a person happy.'

Think about it...

We have been sold this idea of 'perfect eternal love'. And if it is less than perfect then we must fix it. And to fix it there is a billion-dollar industry! From cards to lingerie to diamonds to vacations, to perfumes to...the list is endless!

Another issue sometimes is the marriage of our parents that we have seen as 'ideal'. Gail Sinha, an interviewee, made an interesting point during our conversation. She said, 'I grew up in an atmosphere where my parents had a fabulous marriage (because of whatever the equation was between the gender and roles that were followed to the T). If I look back today, I realize that I grew up believing that every family is like that. Not that they didn't have problems or anything, but they were together on almost every issue—whether it was parenting, beliefs, value systems, etc. I rarely saw them fight. If they ever had an argument, it would be behind closed doors. So we never had tension in our house ever. When I compared their marriage to mine, obviously I could not make peace.'

Are we consciously/subconsciously doing the same with our marriage and love?

Love=Soulmate=equation complete

Another idea drilled into us is of the soulmate. We have been conditioned to believe: Lovers have a deep cosmic connection. Once we are connected all else will fall into place, differences will vanish. We are perfect for each other. They complete us as we complete them—they complement us, counterbalance our flaws.

And we are sold. No wonder we are all looking for our soulmate.

The search for Mr or Ms Right can be risky, since it leads us to expect our partner 'to be completely right' for us, to be a perfect fit. One 'hit' (specially when we are really waiting for that 'someone') and it is seen as a soul connection. One 'miss'—a nasty argument, a slightly bigger difference of opinion, and we wonder if we have made a lifetime error. We then live our life in half-measures, regretting the wrong decision. And secretly we begin again the hunt for the Right One.

In the same vein, we search for completeness in others. And end up blaming the other for not making us feel complete. If we look at another to plug our own holes then what we feel for them depends on how good they are at that job. Thus, we take away from them their 'person' and make them ancillaries to ourselves.

Looking for a soulmate

Dr Rajan Bhonsle spoke of the soulmate too but from a unique perspective. He said, 'Soulmate is someone you embark on a spiritual partnership with. Marriage is the only partnership that demands and facilitates intimacy on so many levels—physical, emotional, sexual and intellectual. Passion is a strong drive towards knowing each other. Two people living together, day in and day out, know the other as completely and deeply as it is possible to know another. The world outside the bedroom, even if it consists of children or parents (people we are closest to), can still be privy to only so many aspects. But sharing a bed in which you can have passionate sex or snore, sharing a bathroom and also the puja *asaan* (mat), sharing friends and family, losses and victories, vulnerabilities and strengths, is sharing one's life in all its nudeness and frills. In fact, so transparent is this relationship that even when one thinks one is unobserved, in all probability the partner is only allowing the illusion of it.

'Our partners see us in our extremes—our mood swings and idiosyncrasies, our habits and our penchants. The close proximity of a couple makes it impossible for them to be in the dark about each other for long. In intimacy, there are unguarded moments when the mask slips, and your partner instantly reflects your inner face to you. Thus, the partner is uniquely qualified to give the other a genuine feedback perhaps more accurate than even our spiritual guru, for they have truly seen us in all our *rasa*, whether *Raudra* or *Shringar*. Even *Veer*.'

And the feedback is not optional! I told Dr Bhonsle about the book I had read, titled *Here Lies My Heart: Essays on Why We Marry, Why We Don't, and What We Find There*. One of the writers of the anthology says something interesting about marriage: 'With marriage you have wilfully introduced a witness into your life…and can no longer close the mind's eyes upon uncomely passages, but must stand up straight and put a name upon your actions. Because if you don't, she will.'

He smiled and continued, 'That actually may really work for us for we are much more than what we project or at least think we have the potential for. This "much-more-ness" is perhaps most easily detected by our partners. If we want to grow, they can be our mirrors. Who can we trust to be our correct mirror more than our life partner? Who else can we ask in all our vulnerability, 'Tell me, what do I do?'

'In all religions we recite mantras. That is not just a ritual. When we repeat the mantras after the pandits we actually say that from now on we are committed to spend our life with each other. Not just to earn money, make a home, have children, have sex, but—as our scriptures say—we marry for our spiritual growth too.

'The one thing all relationships do—and are meant to do, I believe—is to challenge and support each person in their self-growth. If we think of relationships this way, then nothing that happens in them is a tragedy. Two people may grow apart. No tragedy. Two people may have struggles and conflicts together. No tragedy. Two people may break up. No tragedy. Two people may be more than two people. No tragedy. The only tragedy is if the people in the situation don't take full responsibility for allowing the relationship to help them grow and mature. That is a tragedy.

'When we have this sense of trust, to me that is when someone turns into a soulmate.' Dr Bhonsle ended.

Think about it...

What if we looked at another not as our androgynous half but a 'whole' with their own individual flaws and strengths, very much like what we ourselves have? As someone who is not here to complete or fulfil us but perhaps as someone with whom we can share ourselves—our pain, our struggles, our victories, our accomplishments, our fears, our confidences. A someone who could lend a shoulder to lean upon, offer timely solace and advice, support and succour, help us to achieve our own potential. When intimacy is shared and trust developed over a period of time, we endow them with the credentials for such a partnership.

What if 'you complete me' is seen from a standpoint of you furthering me rather than you perfecting a deficiency? Growing with you, rather than feeling complete with you. If the person we love has to complete us then our love is in a problematic situation. Expectation alone—from the other—will be counter-productive. Relationships or partnerships are not built on expectations but on conscious and constant nurturing.

Bina Sarkar Illiyas, editor, designer and publisher of *International Gallerie,* a global arts and ideas journal, said to me during an interview, 'You have to be a partner who must help one another towards reaching his or her goals but without breathing heavily into one's own space. You must give space to evolve. In a relationship you must feel light—you must not feel heavy.'

I remember John Updike's *Too Far To Go, The Maples Stories.* According to one of the stories in it, couples have three eyes. There are the regular two and then there's the third eye that belongs to the marriage.

Think about it...

Does being a good fit mean that your relationship will be conflict-free, that either of you will become psychic, that electrifying sparks will emanate throughout the length of your partnership (40–50 years on an average given our medical advances)?

Where there is intimacy there is bound to be conflict.

Chaos of intimacy

Think of the wives of yore. They had their friends for girly chats; their sisters-in-law to gossip with and discuss the goings-on in the family—including analyzing mom-in-law's actions and inactions; brothers and fathers with whom they discussed, understood and planned their monetary concerns; their brothers-in-law to get pampered by. Neighbours and friends of the husband's family would fill in the newlywed bride on the equations in the family, give tips on the likes and dislikes they would have to consider, and so on. They had a convoy of women to help with child-rearing duties. And they had their husbands to snuggle up with. The men, too, had a fleet of people they shared their responsibilities and needs with—all-men clubs, societies, organizations. Till modern times, most occupations were male-only and workplace camaraderie was an often-sought escape from domestic squabbles. And, of course, there were the mistresses...

Today, all our needs are parked with that one lover/husband/wife. All our needs—sexual, emotional, material—must be met by the one and only. We, too, must be the one-stop answer to their needs.

One-stop shop

Dr Salony Priya attributes single or two-child family with extra-doting parents as one of the attitudinal issues in contemporary marriages. She says, 'Emotional skills are extremely important—handling your own emotions and trying to get a sense of your partner's. Now, in urban India specially, we have this new generation of couples with one or two kids. Parents want to fulfil every single need and desire. The underlying theme is instant gratification and pleasure. Besides, these children are seen as the trophy generation—everyone is a winner, everyone is special. This leads to a sense of entitlement, a culture of "I want". The word, "chill" has replaced "accountability". And these kids grow up and marry people (like their own selves) they love and care for, but none can be like the other's parents, fulfilling every need or wish that escapes their lips. They have no patience for waiting—for anything. They have little tolerance. They demand instant results. This generation not only wants it all from one person, it wants *a lot more* from that one person. General statistics is that one marriage affects twenty people. We need to rethink about our entitlements. The need to be balanced has never been more urgent as it is now.'

Never has so much been claimed from one relationship. We lived in involved communities and extended families where religion and elders customarily filled many gaps. Networks and ties were not just expansive but stronger, and people were more interactive in a very everyday, physical sense (not just on FB and WhatsApp). Our modern urbanized lifestyle, our compact living spaces, our tight schedules, our modern penchant for individuation, has perhaps led to the disintegration of these familial and communal bonds. Inevitably then, we must depend on the one sole surviving relationship. A burden which was earlier shared amongst many must now be the onus of a sole individual. Thus, we have elevated love to heroic heights. With so much weight, is it a wonder then that it crumbles so often!

Thus, love has become an all-or-nothing proposition as we expect it to fulfil all our needs and responsibilities. When it can't, it becomes a betrayal or a disappointment. We either sulk and blame the other or move to the promise of the next 'perfect' one.

According to Kurt Vonnegut, none of us can be a hundred people to each other in marriage and maybe that isn't a failure but a reality to be accommodated with the changes in the marriage script and mise-en-scène.

Think about it...

How can one person address all our needs and quirks? We need a jinn for that, not a human. 'Besides', says clinical psychologist Kalpana Khatwani, 'unlike the West, we are essentially a collective nation. In the US or other European, "soulmate" cultures, even when couples come together and marry, each one still has their separate lives in which each does what he or she wants. It's an individualist country. India is a collectivist nation. Everything here has to be done jointly. Everything here has to be done in hordes. Even shopping, they want others to accompany them. In the US, everyone shops alone. We have done well without the soulmate ideology!'

There is, then, no *one* kind of intimate relationship. There are many; many different individuals who join together, who influence each other's lives, who fulfil each other's needs, who love each other... for a day, for a year, or for a lifetime.

Love versus respect

It is in the name of love that we own and tyrannize, bully and persecute, stonewall and punish. We threaten and torture, we strike where it hurts the loved one most, and we show the power we have over them. When the rage subsides (and we feel guilty), we envelope them in our embrace and mouth the elixir 'I love you'. And in our hearts it *must* suffice.

We do not see our inhumanity. If we see it, it's not held in importance—for we love them! It is not that we do not understand the extent of the pain we inflict with our inelegant behaviour. We do! But there is a larger, more permanent truth than the fleeting episodes of disrespect. We not only love them but we are ultimately their well-wishers. Our love is like a pristine white sheet, the tiny small black dots that appear on the sheet over a period of time are the moments of discord. Should we allow the black dots to merge and become overwhelming dark blotches?

Think of three relationships that you cherish (other than your lover, parents and siblings). Do you dare to misbehave or disrespect them as you do with your 'loved' one?

The problem is not that we take our loved ones for granted; the problem is we do not even see the extent of how inappropriate we have been because we love them. It is in the name of love that we are less than well-mannered with our loved ones! Is love, then, a licence for misbehaviour? Shockingly, yes.

Doctor Kushal Jain, a clinical psychiatrist with VIMHANS Delhi said, 'Love is used as an excuse for disrespect. That is intimacy's biggest problem. And you do not even see how you have wronged the person you love because you love them. Love cannot make up for disrespect, at least not for long. If it does, the love itself will be in danger. So far what we have realized by interacting with so many couples is that there is love, but very little respect. And because of that, the conflicts are much more. *Because it's the respect that will hold the love.*'

Professor Ahalya from NIMHANS said, 'Respect is something which has to come from within. But yes, one can work on it. Respect is something in our country which is associated with some of the outer trappings like wealth, status, or position, etc. So when people come for help, one of the things what we do is—we look out for things which are much more intangible—like for example, the person may have an extremely tolerant nature or he might be an extremely tolerant person.'

Think about it...

Marriage is sold as an extension of true love. People shroud themselves in true love as though it will excuse them from a rational analysis of the situation.

While loving another may/may not be in the current state of our mind, respecting the other person always must be.

While we may/may not desire the 'love' of another we definitely want the other to respect us. While we cannot demand, 'I love you and so I deserve your love', we can surely demand, ' I respect you, hence I too deserve your respect.'

Maybe love is just not enough.

Hate in love

Love and hate are indeed impossible to disentangle. Milan Kundera said:

> It takes so little, so infinitely little, for a person to cross the border beyond which everything loses meaning: love, convictions, faith, history. Human life—and herein lies its secret—takes place in the immediate proximity of that border, even in direct contact with it; it is not miles away, but a fraction of an inch.

Do you remember the time you thought everything was perfect in your life? The person you woke up next to, the morning sun from the balcony, the pancakes that you made to see the smile on your child's face, the assignment that you cracked in record time leading to the much coveted 'well done' from your boss, even the chatty session with the domestic help as you offered her some food? You were proud of the little and big things that you have been a part of and helped *be*—home, spouse, children, work—and you had wished for life to go on this way forever.

An hour passes, the spouse wrinkles his nose over something seemingly trivial, kids decide they dislike the pancake, the blaring sound from the neighbour's makes it impossible to enjoy the quiet winter sun, the phone beeps with the boss bringing to your attention an important point you had missed, and the help leaves with the dishes undone.

Not all of these need to happen at once, or one after the other. Even a few of these in intervals can make us feel lost, faithless and a failure. Everything that seemed perfect does not seem good enough anymore, you question your ability and even if you think you are doing your best, you despair in its (in) efficacy. You not only question your happiness, you wonder if you were truly happy just an hour ago!

And in nothing is this polarity more pronounced and magnified as it is in our deep and closest relationships. We swing from loving them with all our heart for the meaning and purpose they bring to our lives, to hating them for the misery they cause us by exploiting that very love; we thank them one moment for accepting the weak and the worst in us, in the next moment, we detest them for hurting us where they know we are most vulnerable. We feel one in the security they provide, bask in its certainty and we sometimes wish that we were not chained as one because it inhibits our growth and freedom as it will inevitably do at times. We share with them our deepest likes and dislikes and we cannot forgive them for the transgressions or indifference on those very likes and dislikes—even if it is as trivial as not buying a nose strip to manage their snoring, for there is never anything small enough to annoy or take offence at.

Very much like Kundera said, what separates us from loving or hating our closest ones over years, is not miles but inches! And we actually live on that edge, rather on this or that zone. Very much like our partners do vis-à-vis us!

As Molly Peacock said, 'There must be room for hate in love…'

Love = transparency

A woman told me, 'I know my husband so well that he cannot bluff me in poker and he knows my body moves to the last twitch, for the moment I see the nuts in my hand and ruminate on how to bet, he chucks his cards with a chuckle. We wink as we try to "up" the others on the poker table. Once home, we match notes and pat each other for the right read. And then we shudder! What if we could see all else too that was going on between our ears?!

'I think of the man I found handsome across the table and take a peek at him. My husband is still rattling on about the game. I pray to god for the mercy. Sometime later I get to know he had thanked god too for the very same mercy. Naah! I had not noticed that he was fascinated by the pair of legs at the dinner last week. Once I am done with my frowning, we laugh our heads off. We agree that we would like to keep things that way.'

But for many, love means total transparency, the more the intimacy and depth, the more transparent the lovers ought to be. Nothing must be off limits—thoughts and feelings, desires and fears, fantasies and insecurities, schedules and plans, to-dos and not-to-dos. There must be wholesale sharing. Information is connection, knowing is security, confession is curative. Honesty is its guiding star.

And so phones and emails, calendars and appointments, diaries and notes are proudly shared or kept within access. The realm of mind and heart becomes shared territory. We believe love is a merging of personalities.

Think about it...

What an impossible ideal it is. Besides, do we really need to know or be known by each other to such an extent? Remember the times we have wanted to kill the person we love! Or the times we called up our girlfriends and set off on a tirade against them! What if they heard or knew every word we spoke about our loved one?

We belive in complete transparency!

Surely there must have been times when they hated us too! *The Secret Lives of Wives* author Iris Krasnow wrote after interviewing some 200 women on their long-time marriages, 'I am constantly reminded of the eggshell-thin line that separates loving from loathing.'

Would we want to know about those? Molly Peacock says, 'There must be room for hate in love'. Yeah! But do we really need the nitty-gritties of that hate?

Marilyn Monroe accidentally read in Arthur Miller's diary (her then husband). 'Perhaps I had made a mistake in marrying Monore'. Marilyn never overcame the pain of that unwitting revelation. That, it is said, was the beginning of the end of her relationship with Miller.

We are complex, we are ambiguous. We have parallel truths. We have opposing compulsions. We can be communicative, we can stonewall. We can be stingy, we can be generous. We can be as disciplined as we can be crazy. We can love with as much ardour as we can hate—oftentimes the same person! Our world is not black and white—nor are we!

It is not a right to know another person's thoughts. It is a privilege. It's not something we're owed; it's something we're granted based on trust. I think spouses today have the idea that it is their due. To tell one's spouse the truth and nothing but the truth, as one would do in a court of law, is to subject him/her to an unbearable pressure.

Besides, think of the times when we surprise our own selves by behaving contrary to how we thought we would. 'I had no idea I felt so strongly' or, 'I did not know what he/she meant to me till I pushed him away' is something we have all mouthed and heard.

And how boring we would become to the loved one 'all known', how boring the loved one would be to us! Mystery is an essential ingredient in maintaining interest over time in our partner. To be able to feel that there's always more to my lover than what I already know. Stephen Mitchell, in his book *Can Love Last,* addresses the same dilemma. He says, 'In our unions, we endlessly strive to create the safety, permanence, and predictability that we had, or wish we'd had, in our childhoods. However, it's this intense pursuit of ultra-safe relationships that can lead to a loss of spontaneity and freedom, which may kill desire.'

The human impulse to say 'mine' in the sphere of love is

very strong. But it is not our right to know another person's thoughts. It's a privilege, one we must use wisely, whether in asking or dispensing of it.

Dr Rima Mukherjee, a practising psychiatrist in Kolkata, talks about the lopsided transparency in a typical new-age love marriage. She says, 'People who marry put their 100 per cent into the relationship and begin with all the right things—commitment, positive mindset, in love with each other, etc. Both think that things will work out as the two are sincerely putting their best. But the quality of relationship that they have as boyfriend and girlfriend is obviously different than what they wake up to with marriage. Suddenly, from a relationship where the two dreamt of each other as soulmates even when they slept separately, they wake up to practical issues of living together—which, as opposed to the earlier dreamlike state, seems very harsh. From having to handle in-laws (even the ones managing their son's household from long distance) to balancing house and work, to friends of other genders! Suddenly from putting on your best behaviour to finding faults, from being tactful and diplomatic to showing your worst mood swings, from wanting to be totally transparent to not even hearing what is being cried out at the top of one's voice— these result in a huge communication gap.

Initially, they try to correct it but in my experience I have seen that often they concentrate only on what they are saying, and not listening to what the other is, because the other is not listening to them! Soon they start fighting about the other not listening. So on one side they have this need to know each and everything about the other, and on the other side they are not even listening to what is actually being said by the other person! Eventually, they do the math, 'Why speak, it leads to bickering' and they start sharing with another... in some other space! And now they have someone to talk to and they want to be transparent there, not at home!'

The two extremes

We will hurt the people we love; conflict is a part of intimacy.

We will lie, we will yell, we will cheat. Cloaked in silent fury we will feign indifference, we will stonewall and we will criticize. In the face of our needs and insecurities, we will extract revenge by betraying our partners; confronted or confronting, we will fling the betrayal in their faces and accuse them of being the cause. All of us have places where we are raw and weak and are prickly about them. They are the deep-seated wounds we inflict and receive, which cumulate over time. When chafed, these wounds evoke sharp and cruel responses; we hurt with all we have. Because, we can. In these extreme moments we damage what we cherish.

Intimate relationships face the impossible—the paradox of feeling aggressive and loving towards the same person. This is the dance of human relationships and also its everyday tragedy. While we crave to love and be loved, we are also wired to hurt.

Irawati Karve, in her interpretive version of the *Mahabharata, Yuganta,* makes this point quite tellingly. Gandhari, Dhrithrashtra, Kunti and Vidur adopt vanaprastha and leave the riches of the kingdom for a simple life in the forest. Dhrithrashtra tells Gandhari he knew all along why she opted for the blindfold. It was not an act of extreme love but of spite; her rebellion against the injustice of being betrothed to a blind man. Dhrithrashtra says, 'Really, you have punished me severely, Gandhari. I didn't think so at first; at the wedding ritual when you stood with your eyes bound, I did not take it too seriously. I thought that I would plead with you and be able to extinguish your anger with my love. But that was not to be. At night when you came to the bedchamber, your eyes were still bound, and you came stumbling, clutching someone's hand. I was born blind. I had become used to moving about without seeing. But you had deliberately covered your eyes. Your body was not used to blindness. What a horrible night!'

Gandhari admits her guilt with her eloquent silence. Dhrithrashtra, too, owns up to his own cruelty by proceeding to tell her that once the children were born he knew all she wanted was a simple order from him to take the blindfold off, which he would not give. He says, '... by that time my heart too had hardened. I had a kind of revengeful pleasure in knowing you would never see the faces of your sons. Going around with your eyes bound you were playing the part of a devoted wife. You were chained by the results of your own actions. Never again could you open your eyes of your own accord. You could only have done it by my order. And that I would not give.'

Both weep. He gently tells her to remove the blindfold. It is time they both ended this game of hurt. Gandhari does so. A few days later the forest catches fire. Drithrashtra smells it first. He commands the others to rush to the river and cross. There is not enough time to guide the blind old man to safety; he insists they try and save themselves. Gandhari refuses, and taking hold of her blind husband's hand, walks with him towards the conflagration.

This is love's curse as it is love's boon, the extreme hurt and care from the same person. And this is the everyday living of love. You sear your lover over his vulnerabilities, as he does you. Because we love him so much, we can inflict great hurt, and we do. And with him, it is likewise. You proceed to balm him with passion and care. And he does likewise.

The act of hurting the other does not undermine the act of loving. Perhaps this is, at least to some extent, the truth in marriages: You will hurt when you can, but then you will also nurture when you need to; you will damage but you will also build. That, is the paradox of love.

Think about it...

Love's challenge is to withstand the extremes. To be able to say, 'I do not like you at this moment.'

In *Parerga und Paralipomena* (Greek for Appendices and Omissions), published in 1851, Arthur Schopenhauer created a parable on the dilemma faced by porcupines in cold weather. He described a company of porcupines who 'crowded themselves very close together one cold winter's day so as to profit by one another's warmth to save themselves from being frozen to death. But soon, they felt one another's quills, which induced them to separate again. The porcupines were 'driven backwards and forwards from one trouble to the other,' until they found 'a mean distance at which they could most tolerably exist.'

I'm somebody's porcupine. So are you.

Eternal recurrence

In simple terms, eternal recurrence means that everything we are feeling now, we have already felt at some point before; everything we know now, we have experienced in some way before. And so, things keep turning like a wheel, between forgetfulness and remembering.

There is motion, endless motion; there is repetition, unceasing, un-exhausting. Only one thing seems constant, change. There is ebb and flow, in everything within this system and in the shunya outside of it. How we are fated to repeat our actions, vis-à-vis our loved ones over and over again. Nietzsche in his *Will to Power* says, 'That a state of equilibrium is never reached proves that it is not possible.' There is no permanence, no duration, no 'once-and-for-all'.

There is a natural ebb and flow in relationship, a movement between intimacy and distance. Attachment and connection, followed by detachment and disconnection. Up and down, back and forth, give and take, push and pull.

There will be times when two people in love move from 'cannot-live-without-each-other' to 'cannot-stand-each other' to just about tolerating each other enough for the home to run smoothly. And then there will be times when the two simply co-habit the space as amiable friends, filling the roles where the other lapses. There will be that month of passionate amazing sex and then a series of average ones and then some that you really fought hard to keep awake during, and then there will be times when the two involved are too busy with their individual duties to take notice of each other. There will be times when the goodwill runs high and big misgivings are condoned with a mild warning, and there will be times when anything you say will be the spark that starts an ugly long fight. And the power sharing will shift, constantly. Power and awareness change as relationships change and different dimensions of power emerge and recede. Like Jodi Picoult said in her book, *Mercy*:

> You know it's never fifty-fifty in a marriage. It's always seventy-thirty, or sixty-forty. Someone falls in love first. Someone puts someone else up on a pedestal. Someone works very hard to keep things rolling smoothly; someone else sails along for the ride.'

In our intimate relationships once we are 'happy' we want it to be 'for all time'. We want a lockdown. We desire stasis! We try and freeze the settings. Either way, it is a death knell. Life is ebb and flow. When a doting mother fondly tells her cute toddler not to grow up, she knows she means it but for a moment. We accept the fact of children coming close, moving away and coming closer again. We accept friends distancing themselves and then reconnecting, we accept this ebb and flow with our parents, siblings, and most of our other relationships as an inevitable part of life and living. But in our intimate relationships, this scares the hell out of us. We can't accept it and most of us find it impossible to deal with it without creating a scene. We use saam, dam, dand and bhed to fight for stasis. We cling to the ones drawing away, judge them, use emotional blackmail, threats, and social control. We use every trick in our hat to fight the ebb. We fear what is receding will not flow again. When we are the one moving away, our partners do the resisting. We do not have the faith that the lover or spouse who begins to drift away will not keep drifting off forever.

Dr Kalpana Khatwani said, 'I read a book called *Seven Phases of Marriage.* It speaks of the marriage moving through different phases. The first is when the two are joined at the hip. And then the second one is coming to know the real person which means a lot of angry and difficult feelings that need to be processed and worked out, perhaps even moving away a little. The third phase is understanding the other, accepting the other to some degree at least, yet being their own person too; the man goes to conquer—the Yan principle; the woman is busy in nurturing, taking care of the house, children, fulfilling her Yin. Her career, even though important, does become secondary to some level, most often at least. In this phase there is space between the couple, for practical reasons. The next phase happens when the children grow up and leave the nest—the couple then once again is forced to come together and experience a gap regarding each other. They move away and come together once again with the children's wedding or a death in the family. So there is a constant macro cycle, too, in a couple's life. Like they say, the only constant is change. Yet, these are general principles; every couple is different, but marriage is ebb and flow!'

Think about it...

When couples go through tough times they tend to think it's just them. Facebook posts and weekend parties are never really about the tough times that the couple faces, are they? We see only the 'happy' zones. I watched a movie in which a man on the verge of divorce is shown an album by his father. The father tells him that what the son sees in those pictures are the 'happy times', 'the smiles' but that is not the 'whole reality'. There are the 'in-between' stages, the 'downturns', the troughs, that do not get recorded. But they are there. And so, very much like going through another's album, we see the half-truths from the outside and judge our own troughs too severely. But what makes the transition from one 'happy' phase to the other is how two people in love manage their 'unhappy phases' or the troughs! It is the ebb and flow that lasts and makes for fat happy albums.

Try and share this to-and-fro with others. More often than not, they will not only identify with it in their lives but will be surprised at how something so intuitively true is so well hidden and lost behind the haze of 'happily ever after'!

The great gender issue, getting graver by the day

In the book, *The Normal Chaos of Love*, Elisabeth Beck-Gernsheim and Ulrich Beck say:

> The issues dividing men and women are not only what they seem to be, i.e. issues dividing the sexes. They are rather private signs of the crumbling of a whole social framework ... In that respect industrial society is dependent on the unequal roles of men and women. On the other hand these inequalities contradict modern thinking and give rise to more and more controversy as time goes on. The more equal men and women actually become, the shakier the foundations of the family (marriage, parenthood, sexuality) seem.

When it comes to gender inequality, we know, everyone knows, that as a country, India fares rather miserably.

This doesn't speak well about our treatment of women, does it? And not just in the social structure but also when we break it down to our more personal relationships as well. Whether it's the adoring grandmother in whose eyes you can do no wrong, the ever-sacrificing mother who puts you on a pedestal, the sister who has been taught from birth to look to you as her protector or the wife who is expected to cater to your every need, women seem to exist only in the fringes of all their important relationships, without any identity of their own. And nowhere is this uneven balance in the man-woman relationship more apparent than in a marriage.

And then there's the modern woman. The well-educated woman who has been taught to stand on her own two feet; who has been encouraged to follow her heart and chase her dreams; who has been told that she can do/be anything she wants to. The problem is the men missed the memo and are now clueless how to walk alongside their partners in harmony. As Dr Pratima Bhattacharya says, 'It is a gender issue... We want to get our daughters married and get equal status, but we are not teaching the men to give equal status to the women—if the brother comes home from work we ask the sister to make tea or coffee. If the sister comes home from work, do we ask the brother to make tea or coffee? There is a problem in raising kids itself.'

'Though the mothers today try and give equal opportunities to their daughters there is no corresponding growth between fathers and sons. Their father did not speak to them about gender equality and neither did their grandfathers to their fathers. Hence, there is a gender lag,' says Professor Jani. 'And the moment a progressive girl enters a marriage, she somehow finds herself in a patriarchal system which causes a lot of conflict because it is so different from the environment she grew up in. Today we have two distinct kinds of romances, the pre-marital and the post-marital. The conflict comes in the post-marital because of this cultural lag!'

So the problem starts with the upbringing itself. Move a few steps into the marriage scenario and the issues just get more complicated. The fact is that the shell of marriage has changed breathtakingly in the post-liberation era, yet, the soul of marriage—its dream, ideal, ethics and rules—hasn't necessarily evolved to keep up.

Marriage counselling is at an all-time high, and conversations with those in this profession reveal a worrisome picture.

Dr Rima Mukherjee does not mince her words when she states that men 'are a very, very confused lot. They continue to be brought up in a very pampered manner, and almost every family is still very patriarchal. We hardly come across a family or a boy child who has been told that if, in today's world where we are talking about equality, the boy has a working wife, then he should be self-sufficient at home and help his wife with the chores. Instead, the mother still continues to pamper the male child and the mother-in-law still believes that even if the wife is working, it cannot interfere with her household duties.'

'By and large', Dr Mukherjee continues, 'men still have not evolved to the extent where they are able to handle a progressive woman with very liberated views. And there also are huge double standards: What is sauce for the goose is not sauce for the gander. It is okay if he does certain things—if he has a lot of girlfriends, or if he wants to go on a night-out with buddies (even if they are male buddies), and if he returns home at two in the morning, then this is not supposed to be considered wrong by the wife. But she cannot do the same.' Continuing with her thoughts, Dr Mukherjee observes, 'On both sides, the expectations have increased. Theoretically, men are happy getting married to working women but they are not able to handle the consequences. For example, they are not able to handle the fact that the wife is not like their mother who was a housewife—always present to provide him everything, give time to children, manage the house nicely so it looks good, etc.'

She does state that men who have grown up seeing their mothers go to work are far more used to independent women and may even be self-sufficient in several household areas.

The confusion that men seem to face is not an isolated theory. There is also a feeling of helplessness, or rather, cluelessness when it comes to this radical notion of treating women as their equals and that could stem from the fact that it is an alien concept to them; they have never seen it being practised in front of their own eyes.

As Dr Saloni Priya notes, 'The issue that men face is that they have (also) looked at their role in a marriage as a provider—so they feel that they have given her everything. Their conventional norm as a husband is that they are supposed to be a provider. "I have given her a car, I have given her a driver, I have given her money, I have given her freedom, I don't know what her problem is. She only cries, she only cribs."'

'Many times I have seen that the husband is clueless to the emotional pain which the woman has.' Dr Neeru Kanwar adds, 'Men are going through a crisis which they are not being able to resolve—he feels that his role was of a provider but now that role is also not needed as the wife is providing for herself. His role was of a protector, but now he may not be that macho that he is able to protect. And his role was to be the sexually aggressive one, now that also is not needed—so then what is his role? So men are not being able to resolve these crises.'

So what happens when men feel as if they are being bombarded by the 'emotional inconsistencies' of the women in their lives? When they can't take the 'constant cribbing' anymore? When they feel as if their traditional roles have been squashed to a mere shadow of what they were used to? The answer is often not palatable. They turn to another. Adultery is on the rise. And to be fair, it's not just the men. Women, too, often feeling an emotional disconnect from their men, turn to other arms for comfort. Dr Priya confirms, 'Earlier the men were doing it and they felt it was accepted, however, today the

women are also doing it and the issue is the same—they feel that they have been taken for granted; that they have not been appreciated; that they have no identity.' What is the resolution? The solution? How do men and women reduce the gender lag and get on the same page?

To begin with, we have to first and foremost step out from the compulsion of seeing the relationship either as all good or all bad. It is a place where willy-nilly the long-standing differences between men and women are bound to come to the surface. Perhaps all we do have in the end is keeping the lines of communication open and articulating one's wants, desires and expectations.

And, as Dr Mukherjee puts it, 'If you are married, there has to be a degree of adjustment on both sides.'

3

Chaos in Sex and Sexuality

I still remember that one song from *Maine Pyar Kiya* which was Barjatiya's veiled glimpse of 'the desire' in the lovestruck couple: '*Mere rang main rangne wali pari ho ...*' The hero hesitantly shows a picture in a magazine to the heroine, depicting a model draped in a silver-coloured flowing fabric that exposed far more skin than we were used to seeing those days in a commercial family drama; showing skin was a way to communicate sexuality. The hero hands her the 'dress'. As the song plays, the two dance to the number and the heroine gingerly un-envelopes the sheet and reveals herself to the hero, but not to us viewers. All that we viewers were privy to was the lust in the awestruck hero's eyes. It lasts but moments. Then 'noble' love takes over, with the hero respectfully wrapping her up in the flowing fabric. The heroine dissolves in his arms and we, the audience, laud the hero's honourable action and the winning of righteous 'love' over base 'lust'.

I was seventeen then and once more I had seen it stamped! 'Desire' was wrong, lust was something to be hidden and tamed, acceptable only behind closed bedroom doors and in marriage.

Socially responsible movie-makers could afford their audiences the briefest glimpse of base lust and always had the hero of the movie overcoming it heroically, abandoning the unruly path and choosing the rightful moral way. Such tacit messages were commonplace in the cinema and in the social milieu of those days.

The heroine? Well, the woman's sexuality had never been an issue. Said, unsaid, we knew that her sexuality would have to follow the hero's dictates; on her own she would want nothing other than respect and to follow the mores.

Noble love

And once again, in my young impressionable mind, love became synonymous with decency, boundary, respect, control, altruistic consideration and non-selfish behaviour. Passion, (an integral part of a man-woman relationship) was understood as the Satan that had to be endured with the nobler, higher, love.

Today, having experienced life in its various hues, after having read countless books and dissertations on the subject, after having interviewed various experts in the fields of sexuality and psychotherapy and at a personal level with people sharing their stories, I can say with some amount of certainty that 'desire' is a lot about the exact opposite! It is about aggression and objectification, it is about transcending boundaries and claiming power, it is about submitting to power and deriving pleasure from it, it is about being selfish (in turns), and to a large measure it is about being non-respectful. Power and control, dependency and vulnerability, though could be regarded as sources of conflicts in a relationship; but then these become desirable when manifested in the body in experiences of eroticism. The protective and affectionate feeling of love and care, in turn, is an impediment to erotic pleasure.

And thus, a decision was once again being made for me within the mass audience of Bollywood cinema—that even when in the thrall of the exciting world of romance and its accompanying (natural) passions, to love is 'right' but passionate desire/lust is not. Experiencing desire/lust is acceptable, but 'conditions apply'.

I have often wondered about 'desire' and 'passion'. Why does the body change its preference over time? How does love, from igniting passion, become its douse? Why does the body not want what it has? Why is the forbidden so erotic? Why does passion inevitably turn rebel against the status quo, the approved systems, against the mores of society?

I am plagued by questions such as why does society fear the expression of desire so much, why does it panic over its potential reach, its influence? Why is it censured, judged down, left for the anarchists to delve into? How do passion and eroticism interact with society? Are they at loggerheads? Why do the rules say one thing and the body another? Who is right? What is right? And, more importantly, is there a right? Is it possible for a third party to understand and stand in judgement on the nuances of two consenting adults involved in an act so intimate? Is it possible for the two parties involved to communicate a sense of rightness or wrongness wholly and clearly to a third person not part of their experience or relationship? Is this entire arena not too dynamic, too intimate, too complex, conflicting and confusing, too uncontainable, for even the two involved parties to make sense of, let alone for a third or a fourth or an entire society, perhaps for even the law?

But then, there is the family, children, the warp and weft of the fabric that we call society. And then there is this journey of sex and sexuality, first an exploration of one's own body and subsequently a conjoining with 'other(s)'. It is a journey we embark on for an entire lifetime, enjoying it in parts, suffering it in others and being indifferent to it between the two. Who do we look at to understand, to get a sense of context, or for direction? Ancient texts? Societal mores? Law? Religion? Teachers? Experts?

Contexts change, religions metamorphose, laws amend, societies transform, different experts arrive at conflicting conclusions. Premarital sex was frowned upon fifty years back in India, now it's widely acceptable. Masturbation was seen as harmful and unhealthy, leading to impotency; now it has become an accepted safe practice for sexual satisfaction. Things that were once regarded as taboos—condoms, after-pills, Viagra—now comprise a big and lucrative chunk of the advertising industry, reaching out to everyone from cities to tiny villages. From a culture of desexualizing the body, we have now moved to offering an entire range of services—breasts implant, face-lift, liposuction, penile-enlargement, and other cosmetic surgeries—which openly endorse the new era of desired/attractive bodies. From sex as a duty we now have sex for pleasure and not just as 'men only' privilege. The presence of increasing numbers of gigolos/male escorts/male masseurs/male sex workers for unmarried/married women of all age groups suggests a far greater understanding and acceptance of female sexuality than ever before. From arranged marriages to marriages for love, from marriages for love to live-in relationships or open marriages, swinging, homosexuality, man-woman relationship and its associated sexual inferences have undergone massive transformation.

Sex and sexuality

Sex and sexuality cover a wide gamut—from an instinct that demands the experience of pure physical pleasure, to sexual orientation and preference; from how we feel about ourselves sexually, to ways we choose to express these feelings with the self and others; from sexual attraction rooted in erotic desire to the sexual act executed as a matter of habit or duty; from seeing sex as an identity of our gender to how we use it as a tool to negotiate power and control in our partnerships. Sexuality encompasses many ideas and has many facets. And it is forever undergoing change.

Yet, there are certain universals—our obsession with it along with a sense of lack of control regarding it, our fascination with the forbidden and our dwindling desire for the familiar, our sexuality at loggerheads with our domesticity, the desire for the erotic and the tacit taboo relating to it. As real as the soft feelings of love are, as real as need for the social structure that we all are a part of is, is the uninvited spurt between our legs and the stories they tell us regarding our passions. Christopher Ryan in his book *Sex at Dawn* says, ' To see ourselves as we are, we must begin by acknowledging that of all Earth's creatures, none is as urgently, creatively, and constantly sexual as Homo sapiens.'

We are all sexual beings and there is no running away from that. Everybody has a story to tell. So does every 'body', and the story told by the human body is rated XXX.

Sex is not just about the now, the intense pleasure of the physical; it is also about the incomparable feeling of emotional self-fulfilment and connection, even if in flashes. Sex is not just about feeling alive from every core of your cell, it is also about the thereafter; we triumph mortality through our children, don't we? Sex is not just about giving and receiving, it is about sharing oneself unmasked. Laying oneself bare, without the space and the option to accommodate falsity. There can be no sustained lying in the intimate act that sex is; if you are aroused you cannot hide it, if you are not aroused you cannot fake it! People wittingly/unwittingly reveal themselves through the act, in the small gestures and in the big ones. They expose their vulnerabilities and their perspective, their generosity or meanness, their beliefs and ethics, and their strength and their baggage. A friend once said, 'If you want to know someone, sleep with them'. Another I interviewed said about her husband, 'He would go and wash himself the moment we finished. Did he consider me dirty? Or the act? Isn't the time right after sex, one most open to intimacy and sharing? I have never been able to get over the "wash-up-and where's-the-remote-darling" bit. But yes, I must say that this switch-on-switch-off mode, I have understood over the years to be an intrinsic part of his personality. How much does it bother me and what I would want to do about it is a choice I have to negotiate.'

In this intimate act people unwittingly reveal different layers of their personalities too.

Sex is about assertion, what one decides to give-in on and what he/she stands ground for. Sexuality teaches us, more than any other human experience, about self—who am I and why do I exist? In this sense, sexuality is the source of some of our greatest fears and embarrassments. At the same time, it is the source of some of our greatest moments of ecstasy. And it is about expression, where one is in respect to the other. The essential elements of sexuality are self-disclosure and pleasure. Self-disclosure refers to knowing the other, and not just in terms of the others' physical body. Sex is communication, not just about the individuals themselves but also the 'us' they form which is a separate entity by itself. We may say 'I love you' with all the force in our words but what we do during the intimate act is what we feel and when we feel that we love, there is no other language better than the act of sex to express that. The glorious sense of specialness that two people feel as they accept and are in turn accepted in this highly intimate act is one of the rare emotional and psychological highs that we humans have been blessed with.

'Can you think of a greater and a sharper pleasure than love?' 'No, nor a madder one'.(*The Use of Pleasure,* Foucault)

And then, it has so many other obvious benefits too. People with active sex lives live longer. Sex releases stress, boosts immunities, helps you sleep and is heart-healthy. And sex gossip is the foundation on which many friends take their relationship to a much deeper level.

And even when it is not about ours, we are curious about the sex life of someone we know, even if it is not about someone we know, we are curious about the erotic and sexual activities of someone we know who knows someone. And if nothing else, we would still like to know about a person and his sexual quirks even if he/she is a complete stranger.

Sex stories are never boring and they are never just about themselves; somewhere, somehow we link it to our experience of it. And they stay pertinent, across our lifespan, right from puberty till we breathe our last.

We have always celebrated pleasure

The pleasures of sex, the thrills of sensuality, have been explored since ancient times in India—till the Mohammedan and European invaders pushed such esoteric thoughts behind the medieval veil. Manuscripts to folk songs, paintings to dance, statuary and idols—all bear witness to this exploration. The human body has been celebrated for beauty and its great capacity for pleasure. We are the land of Kamasutra and Khajuraho!

During the tenth to twelfth century, some of India's most famous ancient works of art were produced, often freely depicting erotic themes and situations. The best and most famous example of this can be seen at the Khajuraho complex in Madhya Pradesh. Built around ninth–twelfth century, its numerous facades catalogue desire. It is believed that the erotic sculptures, amongst them nymphs, with their sensuous poses and pouting expressions are a way of giving importance to well-being and love of life. During the medieval era there was a common belief that having erotic sculptures or alankaras and decorative motifs was protective and auspicious. The images of Goddesses and Gods sculpted on the temple walls represent the many manifestations of the divine Shakti and Shiva.

As Dr Rajan Bhonsle, hon. professor and head of the Department of Sexual Medicine at K.E.M. Hospital said, 'These temples were built more than a thousand years ago and it took over a hundred years to be built. Which means over three generations of craftsmen worked on it, from fathers to sons to their sons. Three generations of patrons supported it. They were not built in the outskirts, but in the heart of the city and they display multiple positions between Shiva and Parvati. It is symbolic of the fact that there is so much possible, a wide range is possible. Sex was studied as a science and presented as an art.'

Kama was considered an essential pillar of social life and perhaps such was the form 'sex education' took those days. Sex was considered a natural and important aspect of life. Women were not associated with temptation but with fertility, abundance and prosperity; the sensuous was seen as an integral part of the sacred. Human form and beauty were celebrated. Censorship by the state or society did not exist.

Sex turned 'wrong'

And yet, today we look at the body and sensuality very differently. From celebration of the erotic we have pivoted towards a stifling silence, treating it as a taboo. What was once regarded as beautiful, and was auspicious enough to be carved on temple walls, became something unclean, something not fit for public display or discussion. What was once an open attitude, turned into ignorance and embarrassment. Whether it was the later Mughal rulers (Aurangzeb and his successors) or the Victorian values that stigmatized Indian sexual liberalism, it was condemned as unrestrained and barbaric.

According to Susan Reed, a dance scholar, local dances were viewed by the colonizers as 'excessively erotic'—the 'love' aspect of local dances as well as their inherently devotional nature were ignored. No effort was made by those coming to our shores to understand our ancient culture. Instead, seeds were sown for the redefining of the term 'sringara', which until then encompassed love, devotion and sexuality quite comfortably. The middle class was under the Victorian Puritanical influence, which strengthened the ascetic ideals of Indian tradition. 'People believed that since the Western political and economic institutions were better, perhaps their moral institutions were also better,' says Sudhir Kakar, psychoanalyst and author of *The Ascetic Of Desire.*

Dr Paras Shah, Masters in sexual medicine, heading the Department of Sexual Medicine and Fertility in SAL Hospital and Rajasthan Hospital in Ahmedabad, and heading the department at Apollo, Surat, expounded to me how in an era without mass media or mass entertainment, with people spending their days working in the fields, they would seek diversion in the evenings sitting in groups at chaurahas (crossroads) or by the temples. 'Every person, from a young boy to an old man would go to the temples. The paintings and sculptures on the walls of the temples, or the nritya (full of shringar ras) and nataka organized in them, also became mediums of communication on sexuality, showing it to be a natural and accepted aspect of life and living. In those days, sex education was given priority and it was given to everyone. When the Mughals attacked, several temples were destroyed and the priority shifted from sexuality to safety (of women). Hence sex education and its open forms of communication were pushed to the corner and in its place veils or purdah and strict adherence to puritanism became the norm. The Victorian morals furthered the death of the great Indian sexuality. We have not regained our unique past since then.'

Prominent movements such as the Brahmo Samaj in Bengal and the Prarthana Samaj in Bombay Presidency aimed to reform Indian lives, both private and public. Whilst they did work on women's education, raising the age of consent, and acceptance of widow remarriage, they also upheld the puritan notion of sex within the marital space.

Today, sexual cohabitation is commonplace but its discussion is shunned. 'Do it but don't talk about it', is our modern Indian view. India prohibits the publication and propagation of pornography (which is commendable) but in the zeal to keep pornography in check, the system also bulldozes the really essential and educational information.

Many sexologists I interviewed spoke of the gross ignorance in matters of sex compounded with the anxiety of performance and a general feeling of taboo in asking for professional help. Prof. Gaurang Jani said, 'Officially, sex education was banned in Gujarat (after a Jain muni opposed it) and Maharashtra.' He shared an experience where he had been invited to Anand, a town in Gujarat for a talk in a government school. The students were IX and X graders. In an effort to bridge the communication gap between the students and their mentors, Professor Jani urged the students to put their most pressing questions on a piece of paper to open a discussion with the teachers. One boy wrote about the obsessive thought of sex whenever he found himself alone. Jani said, 'The teacher offered his solution to the boy, "Don't stay alone". Just then another hand shot up. This boy said that he had thoughts of sex even in his dream, and he asked her what to do. The teacher looked at me and answered, "Read *Hanuman Chalisa* before going off to sleep!"'

The result, as is only to be expected, is a deeply unsatisfying and unsuccessful sex life. Sexologist Dr Shah has come across this even in long-standing marriages. 'Forget about skills, they lack in something as simple as basic knowledge of the act. Once married they are automatically expected to perform at their best. Unfortunately they do not even know the basics. They have had no place to express their curiosity about their own bodies, forget about understanding the subtlety of the opposite gender. We, as a society, have very few organizations, institutions, discourses for sex education, or to learn the art of sex and sexuality. And how many of us would be comfortable to even be seen in a sexologist's office? My clients who have their wives giving them their BP and diabetes pills everyday keep their visits here a secret!'

Dr Shah has seen more than 5,000 patients in his career spanning over three decades. He continued, 'Majority of men think that once they get erections, they have to start having sex—they hardly know what is foreplay. Without foreplay women are not lubricated and they experience pain during penetration. Their interest in sex decreases as they associate sex with pain and the act just being about the men! And perhaps as a tool that fulfills the part of giving an heir. And the two spend years before seeking professional help. They do not associate sex with pleasure.'

Contemporary cultural taboos limit and repress discussion of sexual matters, even between husband and wife. A sexologist I interviewed asserted that adolescent curiosity about sensuality, when accompanied with total ignorance, often resulted in irresponsible sexual behaviour. Today, we are far more exposed to, and influenced by, world currents. Famously, the world has become smaller, or more connected. Ideas flow freely and furiously across borders. Thus, I will now include what some like to term 'foreign influences'.

Moral policing for sexuality has been the most ongoing debate in the country. A few women drinking in a bar in Mangalore were assaulted because 'Indian women' don't drink and it loosens the cultural fabric of Indian morality.

In another case of rape of a girl travelling with her boyfriend in a bus, the men involved aggressively and self-righteously defended themselves by asserting that it was to teach the woman a lesson. This lesson is about women's moral obligation of not being out in public space after 'a certain time', not to be out with 'a man who isn't your husband' and much more. Every year on Valentine's Day, right-wing activists assault, threaten and abuse young men and women in the name of culture and tradition.

Sanjay Srivastava, professor of Sociology, Institute of Economic Growth, Delhi, says, 'The problem is that just like many sexologists, the state, too, believes that there is something fundamental about our sexual selves, and hence sexuality must be policed. '

Adam and Eve ate the forbidden fruit and fell from grace. For all of us who followed, marriage came as a saviour. It sanctified the carnal instincts for it served the higher purpose of procreation and it also institutionalized its expression by restricting it to the two in the union, validated by the state, religion and society. The dark and untamed had been tamed.

Sexual compatibitily

And then the 'love' in marriage brought its own pressures on the 'sex' in marriage.

From the last few hundred years to the recent past, sex in marriage was pretty straightforward with well-defined nature and roles. Procreation was the primary purpose. Double standards prevailed regarding sex and sexuality, based on gender. While the men were considered manlier with voracious sexual appetites that they generally appeased within and outside the marital bed (with prostitutes and servants), women were either virgins or vamps based on their sexual attitude.

Men had 'rights' to the wife's body. Dr Prakash Kothari in an interview said, 'Most men, even today, use their partners as sleeping pills—when their job is done, they just turn around and snore. They don't bother that their partner also needs to be climaxed or satisfied.'

Pleasure in sex was purely a male domain and the male's release was the primary goal. Women were willing but a passive party, participating more out of a sense of marital duty than anything.

In fact, women were not supposed to enjoy sex and often used it as a bargaining tool in their marriages (because they were socialized to do so). What men fail to acknowledge is that it is only the repression, not the absence, of sexual desires that are there in women. The story *Lihaaf* (The Quilt) by Ismat Chughtai (1941) is a masterpiece to understand the sexual desire in women in Indian society, its manifestation and the attitude of people towards it.

Any form of sexuality outside the marriage and family is perceived as a threat to these institutions and religion is used to safeguard these institutions.

Marital happiness = sexual satisfaction for both

Sexuality today has become an important element of modern marriages. Reasons are manifold and integrated. Growing individualization has made personal happiness and pleasure a focal centre of marriage, birth control pills have freed women's bodies from unwarranted pregnancies and given them unprecedented liberty and choice, ideals of equality and individuality have led women to break away from the traditional double standards of sexuality (where women were seen as being sexually desirable rather than sexually desiring, and males as the aggressors) and steered them towards sexual exploration more in tune with their desires and sexuality, which has in turn led to their demanding parity in the marital bed. Sexuality is today perceived as an individual right and a personal choice. Besides, secularization of sexuality and partnerships have diminished the stronghold of religion and opened up opportunities for diverse lifestyles. Women no longer consider marriage a career. Sexual passion has become the brick and mortar of a good marriage. Influenced by the growing power of the media, both men and women think personal happiness to be a primary goal of sexual relations.

Sexuality has become more hedonistic, pleasure-oriented, and recreational, as the role of reproduction in sexual life has diminished. Today, sex and its resulting reciprocal physical pleasure and satisfaction have become the weathervane of a healthy marriage. People entering marriages have high expectations of physical pleasure from their partners. Even if not clearly spelt out, the message is loud and emphatic. Happy couples have more sex; the more sex a couple has, the happier they report being. Sexual compatibility is being increasingly seen as the basis of a working marriage. Sex therapists have mushroomed in every city and town to help people learn and close the sex gap—learn skills, negotiate needs, clock desires, communicate and express concerns to better this pivotal feature of marriage.

India's leading sexologist, Dr Prakash Kothari, in an interview, said, 'A lot has changed in the sexual mindscape of the Indian couple. When I had begun my practice, I hadn't seen a female patient for three years. But today, the female will come and say—"I am not climaxing, do something for me." The men too have given up the "entitled" feeling, they want to work at bettering themselves, be sensitive to their women's needs."

Marital passion is important as never before. We are a society saturated with sexual imagery. Sex in marriage from a duty has today turned into its great 'fix'. If a couple is having mutually satisfying sex, it is understood that all other issues will resolve themselves in time. A sexologist suggested to me that steamy sex often worked as an antidote for some marital issues. Media with its unceasing adverts sell us the 'elixir' by sensualizing everything from paint to juices to colognes to sheets to even morning cereals! Great sex in marriage is the panacea. And to top it all is the number game. There is no ideal level of sexual activity; it will vary depending on people to settings, to cultural and social mores to fitness etc., yet 'regular sex', even if the regular is once a month, is seen as a marker of a marriage on track.

And sex has become a medium for emotional intimacy, where connectedness is the keynote. Sex is seen as a means of showing care which is about meeting the needs of others, and not just self-gratification. Intimacy is today irretrievably linked with sex. Therapists stress emotional intimacy for sexual intimacy and vice-versa.

Besides, sex in marriage is also about checking the 'love' factor in a marriage via desirability. Love presupposes attraction which in turns leads to desire and thus sex. Rejecting sex (often) may be seen as a rejection of desirability and thus love. Sex in this era of romance is not just about sex, it is about the new pillar of union—love! And this omnipotent pivot is essential to marital stability.

We believe in the ideals of individual sovereign will, the right to freedom and personal choice to engage sexually with our partners. And yet we want our partners to not just desire us sexually but we want them not to desire anyone else too! And we live, not only in close proximity with other attractive, fertile adults but we do so in a society that is far more liberal and open than it was. Women stepping out of their homes and joining the workforce; giving rise to opportunities for travel and sharing and concepts like work partner; men and women interacting socially with alcohol lowering their inhibitions; smoothening the rough edges of the rules of puritanism; vacations with couple friends, and global TV shows which expose us to free Western lifestyles; and morality and religion losing their stronghold on the puritanical rules of accepted behaviour between men and women have led to opportunity, temptation and exploration as never before.

Professor Gaurang Jani said, 'Think of the youth today. They work together, are friends with colleagues of opposite gender, flirt, socialize in groups. And then two of them fall in love and tie the knot. Suddenly, now the same couple does not allow the other to meet and socialize with people of the opposite gender. The seven chakkars around the fire suddenly change the parameters for the two!'

Technology and social media apps—texting, sexting, chatrooms and interactive webcams, mails and instant messages; free, fast and easy, at the click of a button from the privacy of our homes, enclosed office cabins, or during commuting hours—has changed the landscape of potential rebels by an unprecedented access to others, potential rebels or not! Online social environments such as Facebook and Twitter introduce hundreds or even thousands of virtual witnesses into our lives. The music we enjoy, the shows we watch, the daily grind and our emotional state just then, sharing that seems innocuous enough, responding to the shares of others passes off as being polite and friendly. A 'like' here, a comment there, a harmless 'share' and they stay in our minds long after we have logged out of our social webs. And then these sites also give us a platform to reconnect with our old friends and acquaintances, the first love or crush, the more recent ex, the one you always wondered about. There's never been another moment in history when we've had a possibility of instant access to anyone who crossed our minds. And we have the comfort of secrecy to keep the details of communication from our partners. The instant gratification, ease and speed of an interaction almost make it feel like it didn't even happen. Opposite sex friendships formed online quickly progress, leading to platonic coffees and lunch dates, the sharing of details of our not-anymore-so-happening-marriage also to full-bloom relationship troubles with the newly-found friend. And we are connected via technology continuously. The emotional association is more often deeper than what we would like our partners to know.

The apps are right there on your phone. Whether it's a future lover on WhatsApp or a past lover on Facebook, you are so close to finding someone who thinks you are wonderful, attractive and capable– all assurances missing in relationship with your current partner. Technology has at least made the dipping of the toe in untested waters far easier.

The line that we cross from sharing personal issues to emotional infidelity to cyber-sex to an actual one, is often a blurry haze. We tell ourselves we never meant for this to happen and yet nine out of ten times it does!

Some websites cater specifically to married men and women who are looking for relationships outside the binds of marriage. Social media minimizes infidelity stigma and social risk too.

Did you know?

One of the most lucrative businesses is the sex trade. No, not female prostitution—that's ancient! A vibrant segment is the sale of male bodies to women clients. Shefalee Vasudev, in her article, 'Male Prostitutes: Aunty's Lovers', comments, 'It is an invisible story which is familiar but not really. It's about desire and sexual passion. About frustration and need. Sex and money. A bizarre cocktail of secret meetings and inflamed ambition. Of young men selling themselves to support a fantasized lifestyle. Of women who find neither sex nor intimacy in marriages.'

The changing role of women

Once upon a time marriage was not considered a 'problem'. It was the natural course of events, and all in a day's work. But that was in the 'good old days'.

It was only with women transcending their 'property' status that the tension between monogamy and promiscuity escalated. For centuries women had few socially acceptable alternatives—they could be docile housewives, devoted sadhvis, monks or nuns; or they could be courtesans, prostitutes, concubines. Women can now force men to choose between possible types of relationships. The double standard of morality is no longer tacitly accepted. Women seek, even demand, the same liberties as men. If men impose sexual codes upon them, they expect men to abide by such codes as well.

Women and sexuality

The ancient text of the Kamasutra acknowledged and dealt extensively with women's sexuality. Ancient Chinese and Japanese texts, too, covered the subject. But till contemporary times it was not a much discussed matter in the East as well as the West. The female sex had remained subservient to their masculine counterparts and were considered little more than men's possessions. In fact, women were actively denied their sexuality! Manifestations of it were considered aberrations and identified with illnesses—hysteria, neurasthenia, melancholia, etc.

We are now in the Information Age. Ideas spread contagiously. Indian media is in no way shy of tackling issues hitherto considered holy shibboleths or not worthy of open discussion.

The genre of erotic literature, directed at the female reader, is gaining new heights with books like the *Kama Kahani* series and with the influx of Western and Oriental erotica in translation.

Did you know?

In the sex survey we conducted on Survey Monkey, with over 300 responses and 64 per cent females, 22.6 per cent of the respondents said that they were not happy with their marital sexual life while 30.1 per cent ticked the box that categorized it as so-so. To the question if they thought that it was possible for a marriage to be happy without sex and just love, an overwhelming 58.3 per cent answered in the negative. And when we asked who intiates sex inside the marital bedroom, 49.2 per cent ticked on 50-50! Clearly sex in marriage today is far more important for women than it once was.

The insubordinate: desire

In theory, the equation is simple and flawless: Society, religion and law propound monogamous marriage and families. Marriage—at least in contemporary times—is about love, and married sex is a declaration of that love. Sex stems from desire. Thus, love, desire and sex are the smooth cogs of the monogamous marriage wheel on which the locomotive of marriage ideally journeys frictionless all the way to Shangri-la. One-man-one-woman-thirty-forty-fifty-years-exclusive-monogamous-consistent-desire—the land of Happily Ever After!

Yet, gaping holes appear! Desire refuses to follow the neat path charted out by the two involved persons and the body behaves as if it has a mind of its own.

Promising to do something next month is one thing, promising to feel one way after 30 years is something altogether different.

Laura Kipnis, author of *Against Love,* says that we carry the weight of 'modern love's central anxiety...the expectation that romance and sexual attraction can last a lifetime of coupled togetherness despite much hard evidence to the contrary.'

Sex, in a long-term relationship, is now rooted in desire. And desire, by its very nature, is insubordinate! It does not care about laws and rules, morality and mores, right and wrong, convenience and posterity. It refuses to cede control. It is a peek at what is 'unmanageable' within us, a feel of our instincts, and in some fundamental way, it is a statement of what we are deep within.

Desire defies practicality. When it has approval, it palls; when it is forbidden, it becomes unbearably exciting. It craves for what it doesn't have; what it does have, it doesn't want! Desire is erratic and whimsical, it refuses to follow straight lines, it seeks obsessively and when it finds what it seeks, it loses interest. It aches when unfulfilled; once satiated it turns cruelly indifferent.

Desire does not follow convention; it conflicts with our understanding of right and wrong. We may even find ourselves attracted to bad boys and mean girls.

We value people who are kind, dependable and generous, but we may get attracted to the bitches, to the Casanovas, to the ones we know will seek an exit after the act. Respect, which is essential to a democratic relationship, becomes an appalling burden in desire. We feel secure in the known, desire stirs in the unknown—we go to lengths to prove our endurance to our partners; desire, by its very nature, is impatient.

Desire thrives on inequality, on excess; rationality and democracy in sex equates to boredom! It asks for subjugation, it offers surrender; it likes the game unfair and mean, even cruel and violent (at times, to a certain degree). It humiliates and in surrender finds 'connection'; it begs to be subjugated and in aggression finds excitement. Remember books on women's fantasies, *Fifty Shades of Grey*, *My Secret Garden*—what made them hits?

Desire is a fever that runs its course, one way or the other. It is that inescapable presence in our lives which refuses to sit neatly on top of love and marriage and all the other systems prescribed and sanctioned by society, state and law. Desire is our biggest blessing and our worst nightmare—sometimes simultaneously!

Desire equals love. Or does it?

A friend I met after twenty years at a college reunion said, 'I know he loves me but I want to be desired! I know he cares for me, but I want to be ravaged in bed, not respected! I can live without the mushy love'.

The sexual impulse is the most fervent of cravings, the desire of desires, the concentration of all our willing. Accordingly, its satisfaction, corresponding exactly to the individual desire of anyone, is the summit and crown of his happiness, the ultimate goal of his natural endeavours, attaining which, everything seems to him attained, and in the absence of which everything seems to have been missed.

Sex, when in a long-term relationship, becomes deeply personal. One not only gives pleasure but, in the giving of pleasure and the knowledge of the beloved receiving it, feels a unique pleasure. Besides, in erotic intimacy we reveal our innermost fears, desires and wishes and in our partners acceptance of our most intimate corners, our shame (that has been impressed upon by society and culture) dissolves. Two complicit in each other's desires and needs become like partners in crime who are one.

No wonder 'to be desired' in love is the ultimate aphrodisiac and validation of that love, for desire is an instinct; it cannot be faked or willed. We know it sources from somewhere deep within us, from someplace that is unsullied, an involuntary hidden corner. We cannot affect it, will it, or even regulate it! Hence, desire in love is that 24-carat gold that we touch upon ever so often in the beginning of our relationship, but are left longing for even as our love and commitment towards our partners deepen. For even if the new science and sex gurus suggest us ways to bring the spark back in our sex lives, there is no guarantee that it will be as high-octane as it once was. Besides, the partners may take this the wrong way and decide that it is a sign of them not being wanted or desirable anymore. Dealing with sex issues within a long-term relationship like marriage is like walking on eggshells; there are more chances of breaking or messing things up.

As our relationship grows and love deepens we expect desire to strengthen and use its presence as the test of love itself. We believe that to be desired in a relationship is the first point of validation of the love in the relationship; we believe that love and desire follow each other like Siamese twins!

But do love and desire originate from the same space? Do they fulfil the same needs? Do they look at the other from the same standpoint? Does good intimacy always lead to good sex? Does the absence of one automatically mean the lack of other? Or conversely does the presence of one presuppose that of the other?

Psychologist Reik in *The Psychology of Sexual Relations* has discussed the distinction in the two languages—that of sexuality and that of emotional intimacy. In sex the quest is physical satisfaction; in love the quest is emotional happiness.

Similarly, in the book *Mating in Captivity*, author Esther Perel states that love and desire function at completely different levels. Perel points out that desire is about wanting to know; while in love there is already a lot that is known and hence, it curbs the desire.

Think about it...

Imagine you met someone at a party and felt that small burst. Did the burst mean love? Then why do we judge our partners so harshly? Have you ever wondered, why is it that the desire of others appears coarse, while one's own is always sublime?

The inconsistency of desire

In the course of writing this book I interviewed many therapists, sexologists and counsellors. According to them, even as care, commitment, companionship, comfort, respect etc.—all aspects of love—deepen as marriage progresses, sexual desire wanes. Low sexual desire for their mate is one of the most frequent complaints heard from patients, especially those involved in long-term marriages.

Dr Paras Shah says, 'It's hard to generate excitement, anticipation and lust with the same person you look to for comfort and stability. Excessive presence kills the strongest passions, takes away the mystery necessary for the erotic. Remember Freud's words? Where they desire, they cannot love; where they love they cannot desire.'

Marty Klein, a licenced marriage and family therapist and certified sex therapist for 31 years, was questioned in an interview about sexuality and desire. Klein answered by way of an interesting analogy—the rational answer to why elephants don't fly is they are not designed to do so. He applied the same logic to monogamy in marriage where we have two individuals who are expected to stay married for decades with a constant desire. He adds, 'The real conversation we need to have is how do we operate as professionals in this world where the entire culture refuses to face its own grief about wanting something that it's not going to have.' Klein further argues that even if we put together a thousand long-term couples, the most common grouping will be the one where either one has desires more than the other, or though both love each other, they don't desire each other, or they both have high desires but then these are not directed towards each other.

This further elucidates the point that desires die in a more familiar, known, long-term association; hence, expectation of monogamy from humans is unreasonable.

There are many reasons that lead to a loss of desire. Novelty is a major sexual stimulant, it is automatic in the early stages of a relationship, but as sex becomes more familiar and less novel, desire plummets. Remember the feeling, been there done that! You know every move of your partner, you understand every moan, you make love in the same bed, overlooking the same carpet, on the same sheet. There is no new place to go... Literally!

Sex is available on call, and it loses the forbidden and erotic quality that is a turn-on. Being pursued, being sought after, stimulates desire. In long-standing marriages pursuit flags and seeking gives way to blasé habit, desire wanes, overfamiliarity results in a decline in the romance; there is less and less interest—or none—in sexual innovation, in caring for one's appearance and physical fitness.

Under the stress and burden of modern living, children, home and jobs, one's need for space and individuality is compromised, which in turn compromises desire. You are one and in control as parents/bread-earners/troubleshooters (loss of one's own sense of individuality), but need to be two with your separateness in the bedroom. Eroticism requires separateness. How do you move from being one to two, the moment the bedroom door clicks shut? And who has the luxury of time to allow the transition its pace! Besides, the roles we are forced to play by our domestic circumstances—that of a wife/mother/professional or a husband/father/son/professional are not just overwhelming but very desexualizing. Resentment, too, is a big desire killer; resentment that occurs in long-term relationships from long-held grudges, dissatisfactions and unmet needs.

Besides, the paucity of desire can also stem from a long list of other factors like depression, stress, past sexual trauma, certain medications and medical disorders.

'The very elements that nurture love—reciprocity, mutuality, protection, closeness, emotional security, predictability—are sometimes the very things that stifle desire. Love wants a certain kind of closeness; desire needs space and distance to thrive,' contends Ester Perel, a couples' therapist. Psychoanalyst Michael Badar in his book *Arousal* shares another exploration of erotic impasse. He describes that intimacy is bound by the feeling of concern for the other person and fear of not hurting. Sexual excitement, on the other hand, is linked to an apathy to such concerns or fears.

Also, though deeply in love, partners are still not comfortable speaking of their sex lives with each other, expressing their needs, guiding their partners to the erogenous zones, helping each other know what they enjoy most.

Think about it...

Have you shared your fantasies with your partner? Dr Prakash Kothari said, 'Once romance fades in a relationship, hormones alone are insufficient to fuel sexual desire.'

And sometimes two people are just a bad fit in bed! The barriers are not just interpersonal. They are personal and biographic as well.

Helen Fisher, an evolutionary anthropologist, states that the hormones responsible for romance (dopamine, norepinephrine, and PEA) are known to last no more than a few years at best. Oxytocin, the cuddling hormone—outlasts them all. She describes that lust is metabolically expensive. She says, 'The fruits of this ripening love—companionship, deep respect, mutuality and care—are considered by many to be a fair trade for erotic heat.'

Another person I spoke to, married for over eleven years, said 'Don't they say, familiarity breeds contempt? I suppose you just get bored with making love to the same person, in the same way, all the time. We still loved each other, but our sex drive disappeared. We put our energy into other things... I think we were both sexually frustrated and it made us snappy with each other.'

What starts as romantic love, passion, and desire for intimacy and love takes a different turn when this association takes a form of permanence, and is supplemented by a series of varied personality negotiations that follow in a marriage. There is much more than the romance that one encounters in a marriage. When one actually encounters the other person's morning bad breath, or the farting, or the untidiness, the desire starts to fade. The other's body ceases to become novel or mysterious. The sexual mores become repetitive, and one can very well foresee and expect what will happen next.

Remember the line from Silsilay, '*Har rishta ek mod per aa kar apni garmi kho deta hai*'. The connection between desire and love doesn't last as long as the need for each. A gradual decline in the intensity and frequency of sex between a married couple is an inevitable fact of biological life, and as such, evidence of deep normality. For most couples, desire varies as relationship progresses; obsessive and enticing in the beginning (like a thousand-watt current), neutral as the two settle down in the relationship, and often recluse and problem-laden as the body gets the monogamous deal of the bargain! This change can be perplexing and difficult to accept. Our society, laws, the religion and media do not help. On the contrary, we are hammered with opposing messages. Marriage should be enlivened by constant desire; sexual desire and peak can be maintained for decades. There must be a want. If at all, the fix is there, we must care enough to ask for it! From biology, desire becomes about the psyche! Yes, the sex-therapy industry is the gainer!

Desire fades... period. It fades because time and success are its enemies. It fades because biologically we cannot want what we already have. It fades because it is meant to. Sex and sexual expression change along with the longevity of a relationship, ebbing and flowing during a lifetime with children, work and other things in life taking precedence over one another.

For most of us, there will be times when sex is great and times when sex is terrible and then there will be times in between the two.

When desire fades

When desire wanes, we conclude love is gone. When we begin desiring another we think it is antithetical to our love for our partners. When we feel sexual boredom we conclude something is wrong with either us or our partners. Perceiving the 'wrong' in ourselves we might conclude we are poor lovers, incapable of satisfying our partners and thus forcing them to seek sexual satisfaction elsewhere. Perceiving the 'wrong' in our partners we might think them loose, immoral.

Next time you are at a party, or a bar, or any of the other bad excuses for festivity that our time has to offer, notice the behaviour of the couples there. See how they can hardly bear to be separated; how they will suspiciously follow with their eyes any attractive person passing by the spouse.

A lady—let's call her Rati—spoke of the time her husband asked her for repeat sex. She screamed at him, accused him of insensitivity, of not understanding that she did not want it right then. She told her husband, 'I don't think I ever want to get into bed with you again.' The husband was crestfallen. She said that she felt that if the thought of sex repulsed her so much, perhaps they were in an unbearably incompatible marriage, with him being sexually frustrated and rejected, and she feeling defective and invaded. She said, 'We were snappy and unhappy with each other but looking back now I realized that it was just a desire gap, rooted, to a large degree, in automatic, biochemical processes that had little to do with how attractive I found him or whether he cared for me. Our body needs were different from our love needs!'

Desire differences are natural and normal

In the fast-changing world, relationships also do not experience the kind of permanency as we would like; everything comes with an expiry date. Sexuality and marriage were never about exclusivity as suggested and discussed in Western literature. The idea of marriage was not bound by the norms of sexual exclusively and fidelity was a much later addition to the vocabulary on sexuality.

Think about it...

Sexual passion is rooted in our natural body rhythms. By the time we have been together for long enough to not close the bathroom door for our daily activities we are likely to find our eyes and fantasies wander. It's not like we want to rip the clothes off somebody that we are sleeping with for the 1,000th time. Yes, marriage is about choice and commitment but that does not mean our senses have to deaden outside that choice.

Nor does it mean that we need to deaden them so as to protect ourselves from their allure. And most importantly, can we really do that? Being in love does not protect us from lust; a ring around the finger does not cause a nerve block to the genitals, the thrill of the chase doesn't disappear simply because you've met the love of your life. No matter how extraordinary we may be, we cannot protect the other from the tedium that comes with time—familiarity, the subsiding hormones and its disillusionments. Besides, we must remember our partner's sexuality does not belong to us.

When we desire another...

When we desire another we think one of the three things:

Something is wrong with us (we are loose, immoral, we do not know ourselves anymore), something is wrong with them (maybe it was really not love after all!) or that something is wrong with the marriage!

Maybe it is time for us to reconsider the supposedly irrefutable connection between desire and love, commitment and sexual exclusivity and its effect on us. Marriage experts estimate that one out of every three couples struggles with mismatched sexual desire; one spouse is hot when the other is not. In desire and sex, longevity is a game changer.

We will desire other people. We will want to sleep with them, but then how many times do people leave marriages just to sleep with someone else and have it come back to the same thing? In the course of this book many said that each time they've considered parting, they've realized that they may find a better sexual match, but not a better life partner. Maybe marriage and love is about something bigger than the state of desire. Maybe it is possible to love someone a lot, but still not be very sexually turned on by him or her.

We can all experience love for more than one person at a time, and will likely do so over the course of our increasingly long lives. We respond by engaging in secret affairs, divorces (serial monogamy) and/or by channeling our frustrations into fantasy (pornography, prostitution). One way of loving someone is to acknowledge that they have desires that exclude us, that it is possible for them to love and desire more than one person at the same time. We all know that this is true, and yet we don't want the people we love to start believing it about themselves.

Sex can be an important part of intimacy, but it is not the essence of intimacy itself.

'I encounter millions of bodies in my life; of these millions, I may desire some hundreds; but of these hundreds, I love only one.'(Roland Barthes, *A Lover's Discourse: Fragments*)

As Erica Jong once said, 'Yes, wild passionate sex exists [...] But it is occasional. And it is not the only thing that keeps people together. Talking and laughing keep couples together.

Shared goals keep couples together.'

There are those nights, rare but unforgettable, which may begin languidly but build up to summits of ecstasy. There are also those nights when, in synchronized singleness, lovers lie stark naked in bed languorously holding hands, without the need for any verbal communication. And there are several intervening nights…

Half-baked knowledge and assumptions

What's the biggest mistakes your clients make? I asked Doctor Prakash Kothari,. 'Assumptions', he said, 'they make assumptions about what the other is doing, feeling and thinking. And they assume that they are supposed to automatically know and what they are doing is right. If you ask me honestly I do not blame them. The awareness has started building, but…'

Think about it…

We are schooled for everything in life. We test the rules of our knowledge, re-examine them and re-learn if needed. We are evaluated and graded and we are encouraged to ruminate on our gaps and guided on how to plug the holes. We are trained, again and again, with love, force, threats and motivation, till we get it right. We sign up for classes, we upgrade our knowledge and skill, if needed, we change tracks, take up a new profession, some of us change yet again till it feels right. In short, we continue learning.

Yet, in sex, we operate from a different mindset, it is as if we are born experts and continue to stay that way! The fact is that most do not even have the basic education of it and expect to know everything automatically or from our peers. We are expected to keep mum about our curiosity or ignorance about it. We are either sex maniacs or simply stupid. We are expected to somehow know it all magically.

Dr Paras Shah says, 'We have no sex education given anywhere today—not even in schools, neither in colleges. Hence people are not even aware of their bodies. Majority of men think that once they get erections, they have to start having sex; they hardly know what is foreplay. Most people think that sex happens only at night, in the dark. Around 40 per cent of couples only have sex in the dark at night, they hardly see their faces or each other's naked bodies in light—even after having sex for years. And because of this, there is no concept of foreplay.'

In fact to be even caught with a book on sex invites glares and looks. I remember reading a book titled *How To Think More About Sex*, by Alain De Botton, while I was waiting for my flight at a café in an airport. The cover had no images, yet as fellow passengers happened to chance upon the cover, I got either smirks or embarrassed looks as they quickly moved their gaze away; one bold fellow actually had the audacity to keep staring at me and when I finally met his eyes he smiled knowingly and introduced himself before glancing at the book as he asked, '*Aap kahan jaa rahen hain*?' Where are you going? He must have thought it was his lucky day; maybe mine too! A nymphomaniac in the waiting room of the airport!

And imagine our system of copulation (for a large majority still) where practically two strangers are supposed to manoeuvre all challenges and be the all-knowing lovers on the famously celebrated first night! Imagine their own ignorance, the unfamiliarity with their partners and no avenue or model to express their own discomforts, issues, in-confidences and problems or listen to those of their partners' for this most natural act.

Case study

Dr Paras Shah spoke of a client who held a high position in a government job and was not able to have children even after five years of marriage. He had carried out some tests too, both on himself and his wife. The tests revealed low sperm count. He was undergoing treatment for it but it had just been a few months and he was getting impatient. Then someone suggested a tantric to him. The tantric told him that if his wife sleeps with her brother-in-law, only then would she be able to have a child or else the couple would stay childless. Dr Shah said, 'The guy was well-educated. I told him that I would give him medicines. It would take some time because the sperm count cannot go up in a day. But the guy never came back to me. People lack even basic knowledge on sex in our country.'

Perhaps, in the beginning, the hormones do fill the gaps but what when the novelty of a new body and the act wears off? What when desire loosens its grip and the play of biology kicks in? What when the excitement levels drop as they are bound to? What when 'been there, done that' and the attending boredom stands at loggerheads with the 'I will always love and desire you'?

I conducted a survey on how many couples do actually visit a professional to address the sex issues in a long-term relationship. What do you think it said?

In our sex survey, 93.7 per cent of the respondents said that they had never been to a counsellor or a sexologist even when they had issues in their sex life!

I asked Dr Paras Shah what issues males generally reached out for help with. He said, 'Most men do not have proper knowledge of a woman's body and some even question their own libido.'

Add to this the omnipotent standards of sex continually fed to us—what constitutes sex (penetration); what signifies that it is done (orgasm of at least one partner). How much sex is 'normal'; how intense should it be? How long do most men last during intercourse? What is the frequency of orgasm? What's the level of performance? How intense is it ? What's the desire quotient? Has it sagged? Then it must be worked on. Unblock the natural libido (a huge industry exists on how to achieve that and the industry has already sold us the normal sex average).

And then we have the sex facts (whether they are true or not)—men desire sex more than women.

Though sex is a private matter, its norms are very set. Even though many magazines, newspapers, TV shows, soaps, art, books, etc. sell the art of sex and speak of getting the zing back, how often do partners have an honest, intimate talk on their sexual thoughts? Do they share their turn-ons—what actions, what body parts, what hidden desires, what behaviours, what outfits? How to pleasure each other more? What are the erogenous zones? Do they share their fantasies? Do they play in the bedroom? What are they doing wrong? What are their concerns and worries? What new thing they can try? Generally, each partner thinks that the way they think about sex is obvious to the other. Nothing could be further from the truth. People don't want other people to know what is going on in their bedrooms. It's scary. Instead, they worry about being judged, or that their marriage is somehow broken.

Dr Paras Shah said that when clients come to him he always asks them if they maintain the service schedules of their vehicle/s. 'Inevitably, they nod with emphasis. "That way we can catch the trouble before it begins," they say proudly. But when I ask them, "What of problems in their sex lives?", Is it because of small children? Stress? Familiarity? I draw a blank. It seems we pay more attention to the upkeep of an inanimate car than such an important and intimate part of our lives'.

Dr Prakash Kothari, too, said that the passion and urgency that characterizes the first few years in a marriage eventually dies down, no matter how great and intense it was. 'Besides', he further detailed from his experience, 'very few women can actually come in the act of intercourse, especially in the missionary position. That is one fact not very commonly known.'

In the sex survey that we conducted this point came across very strongly. When asked what was important for women to have an orgasm, while 58.3 per cent said it had to be vaginal intercourse, 22 per cent said it was not relevant!

Did you know?

Only 25 per cent of women are consistently orgasmic during vaginal intercourse. Whatever the size, however much time it goes on for, whatever her feelings are about herself or the man she is in bed with. This statistics comes from the book *The Case of the Female Orgasm* by Elisabeth Lloyd, after a comprehensive analysis of 33 studies over 80 years on the subject.

According to Kim Wallen, professor of behavioural neuroendocrinology at Emory University, 'Simple physiology may have a lot to do with orgasm ease—specifically, how far a woman's clitoris lies from her vagina.' Wallen proposed the rule-of-thumb theory, i.e. the distance between the clitoris and vagina. If the distance is 2.5 cm or less (roughly from the tip of your thumb to your first knuckle) it will result in orgasms from penile stimulation during intercourse, while if the distance is more, the women may need some extra stimulant.

So, just as there are physical attributes that prevent one from doing headstands in yoga or becoming a concert sitarist, there are attributes that make it unlikely for some women to ever experience orgasm from intercourse alone.

Think of all those women there who think they are frigid or weird, or less of a woman because they cannot orgasm or that their partners cannot go on long enough or whatever else they may attribute not having an orgasm to! And think of the men who feel less of a man because their women cannot orgasm! Not knowing that the real cause is a physiological one. A person I interviewed said, 'My current partner is frustrated because he's never had a problem making a woman happy until now, and it's frustrating for me because I just don't understand.'

Think of our conditioning—if the man is really a man he would satisfy the women with his penis alone. The man too thinks the same and does not offer any other kind of stimulation. He is not able to take her to the heights but she does not say anything (it may bring his esteem down) and perhaps even fake orgasm. Because she fakes orgasm and does not say anything, he continues thinking all is good while she thinks she is just performing a duty.

Dr Prakash Kothari said to me during an interview, 'Why do we listen only when the West says so? Vatsyayana, in Kamasutra, specially mentioned that if a man is unable to satisfy his partner, then he must satisfy her by oral sex or masturbation. The important thing is satisfaction—not sexual intercourse.

Did you know?

Women, did you know that the intensity of your pleasure is not dependent on the size of his organ? Only about 4 centimetres (external one-third) of the vaginal canal contains sensory nerves for arousal and orgasms.

Men, did you know that for a woman's orgasm, the penis size is not important?

Prakash Kothari was the first person who brought to attention the fact that a man's penile size in an erect stage can be anything from two inches or more and even two inches is enough to stimulate the woman as only the outer one-third region of the vagina is packed with sensation! He said, 'Both men and women think that longer the better, but this is Godzilla logic. What really matters is strength and technique."

Communication is essential

We do not become mind readers in the bedroom. Really, we don't! Despite what is shown in the movies, most of us cannot read minds, and we do not have built-in radar to let us know what our partner's experience is like.

Remember all those math classes you took, the mantra that was drilled, 'If you do not understand, ask!' You asked and it was explained and you worked on it, step, by step and there was this light—you got it! The rules for sex are not too off this simple advice. When in doubt, ask for help, and a corresponding rule for receiving pleasure is 'speak up!'

You think you do?

Take this simple questionnaire to find out:

A. Do you tell your partner what turns you off (that he does) during the act or ask what turns him/her off (in you)? Could be anything, bad breath or unhygienic body parts (Dr Paras Shah mentioned this as one of the major reasons people reject sex in marriage), no foreplay, no experimentation, an unresolved argument earlier in the day etc.
B. Do you discuss what turns you on and vice versa? Foreplay? Lingerie? Candles? Glass of wine? Massaging each other?
C. Do you guide your partner on ways (during or after the act) on how to maximize your pleasure or ask how you can maximize his/her pleasure?
D. Do you discuss your fantasies and your kinks? Do you ask about your partner's fantasies and kinks? Do you discuss about those that you would like to try out with your partner? Does your partner have the confidence to discuss his/her kinks and propose what he would like to try out?

E. Do you say to your partner, 'I want', 'I need'? Does he/she ask of you the same?

F. Do you fake orgasm? (this itself is misdirected communication, means that you are taking the 'finish' line. It is all right once in a while, according to Dr Paras Shah, but if resorted to more often, then it makes the satisfaction quotient, in the long run, poor, thereby negatively affecting the relationship.)

G. Do you read or watch erotica together and discuss new possibilities?

The counter argument here might challenge the need to over-communicate, or you may not want to ruin the 'romance factor'. However, we are addressing the sexuality of the much-married couples here. The element of mystery may work only during the first flush in the marriage bed. As the years mature, communication is a dire necessity to improve and retain your sex life.

Yes, sexual dissatisfactions and turn-ons are hard to voice (than most other issues), they are even harder to receive; besides, the taboo, collective awkwardness and stigma attached to it adds to the anxiety and discomfiture. Yet, what may seem as a conservative, non-conflicted and safe approach can actually create deep dissatisfaction and ensuing resentment where the two blame each other for being wronged when they have not even voiced how they have been wronged!

A person I interviewed said, 'I kept sort of waiting for him to figure it out, and then I'd be frustrated as I bounced between denial and desire, wanting and not having, gratification and repression. And then my frustration would turn into anger because he wasn't figuring it out. I would conclude, "He is selfish. He does not care about my pleasure!" Well, I did not speak up!'

A woman I spoke to said, 'I can scream and moan the amount I want to, but unless my man makes a point of saying later, "Wow when you did—, that was awesome!", I really do not know if he appreciated it or not.'

And that can be quite scary. This lack of clarity about what gets a man going is enough to throw a woman off, who might otherwise, have initiated sex. Anxiety about what really satisfies him inspires some women to simply leave the whole thing up to the man.

Let her know when she does something that feels really good. Speak of what irritates or discourages sexual excitement. Identify what heightens it. Own your desires and your wanting; engage with your fantasies. Take responsibility for your sexual fulfilment. Do your bit. Being direct and open is the key to discovering your own sexual rhythm and of others', and tuning them.

Communication may be based on agreement (i.e., two people having the same opinion on an issue) and understanding (i.e., each person recognizing the other's viewpoint). If you cannot agree with your partner or your partner does not agree with you, at least the two of you will understand and recognize the other's point!

Internet is filled with how to communicate, use it. There are therapists, counsellors, books that can aid you in specific issues; all you have to do is search. But I would like to record one interview where the speaker chose to be anonymous. She said, 'I would write him notes, for instance, "I read about this and would like to try it out tonight, what do you think?" He would come home desiring! Talks do not work for us, notes do.'

While teaching a new trick to a dog, one always gives a dog a treat, a 'good dog' pat on the head, and most people know that this reward helps the dog to learn the trick. But when it comes to human relationship, we forget to do this. So, in bed, if your partner does something you want to happen again, remember to extend the treat to your partner. Murmuring encouraging words, reciprocating by working on his/her hot buttons, a kiss, anything that expresses instantly and clearly that he/she is along the right path can do the trick.

Maybe sex is not about engineering (how to solve); it is a language used to express and understand!

Did you know?

After interviewing marriage counsellors, psychotherapists, sexologists and regular people (via surveys), I got a host of reasons for women not taking the sexual lead in a marriage. Yet there were some that stuck out more than others. One in particular was women's concern with how they are perceived if they did take the lead. Would they not be judged as loose, dirty, sluts? Would their boldness be interpreted as them being seen sexually easy (to other men's passes)? Would their desires make them seem aggressive and selfish, conflicting with the disposition maintained for running a home and children? You can thank society and perhaps even their mothers for this reluctance—'goods girls do not initiate!'

I'll be honest: I've probably initiated sex seven times in my entire life, and at least three of those times, it was the tequila.

According to the experts, nothing can be more of a turn-on for the man than a woman in control. A person I interviewed said, 'He wanted me to want him, and I never really understood what he meant. While he beat himself over with "Is it just me who wants sex?" "Am I failing to satisfy her?" "Is my technique wrong?" I know now how intrinsic to a man's self-esteem is the idea that his wife actually desires him sexually. And here I was thinking the opposite!'

The second-most common reason was that sex hurt. A woman said, 'Not only have I had too much "fast" sex, void of foreplay, but I've had too much one-sided sex.'

In an interview, Dr Paras Shah said, 'What if I served you bad coffee? You would drink it to be polite the first time. The next time around you may accept the cup hesitantly. If the coffee was still bad when you come to me again, and I offer you the beverage again, would you say yes? Naah. You would come up with a host of excuses, "Just had a cup at home, will have water", etc. But it is not just the men who are the culprits here. The women are to blame too. Why is sex charity or duty? It must be fun! They must speak out, ask to be pleasured, show interest, explore your sexuality. Democracy in bed—that's my mantra!'

Dr Kothari says, 'Foreplay starts at least 12 hours before the actual lovemaking. A teasing gesture here, a helpful hand there, a compliment, a flirting glance, the aromatic perfume brush go into foreplay long before the actual foreplay'.

Some reasons that came out for women not making the first move:

Many women use sex as the way to have some control/influence over the partner. It is their brahmaastra! The man appeals and she dispenses. And so she cannot initiate.

She was rejected the last time she initiated.

Counterpoint: Think of the times men get rejected.

It could do with the way one sees oneself. She doesn't like her body. Bum's too fat, breasts not firm enough, pigmented skin, saggy arms, the mirror just does not give the go-ahead to them.

Perhaps women need acknowledgement that their bodies are sensual before they can feel sensual themselves.

Counterpoint: There is no bigger aphrodisiac for a man than to know he is desired. The last thing that men think of is his physical attributes while he is getting an invitation to sex!

She thinks if he hasn't already made a move, he wasn't in the mood anyway. Almost universally in this still male-dominated world men enjoy greater freedom than women. Such female subjugation has led to a lack of self-confidence in women. They are more prone than men to second-guess themselves. Even in the bedroom, the woman may feel like having sex but if she is unsure of her man's interest she will more often than not abstain.

She has less desire than her man. According to the experts, in all the age, ethnic, geographic, and professional groups, a majority of women respondents rarely initiate sex. The deeply ingrained pattern that a woman's sexuality is of less importance than a man's and that female assertiveness in the sexual relationship will not be rewarded, almost ensures an imbalance of desire between the sexes, or, at any rate, perpetuates the myth that there is one.

On the issue of sexual desire experienced by married women, studies support the notion that perceived influence and power affect women's sexual behaviour as well as sexual desire. When women hold less power within the relationship or within society as a whole, they may use or withhold sex in an attempt to mitigate this skewed balance of power, or they may feel little desire for sex in a relationship in which they feel powerless.

Many experts believe that women are the more sexual creatures, only that sexuality has long been repressed. Women can have multiple orgasms where men must have a cooling period after one. Women are the more verbal ones during the act and though they are slow to arouse, once there, they can go on for a much longer time than men. However, a clarification is in order: the *Savitabhabhi* comic strip is hardly the paragon of 'liberated' thinking. In fact, it incorporates the most conservative male fantasies about the 'modern' woman who is forever willing to please a man.

Unfortunately, society at large slut-shames women who are deemed 'too sexual'. These pressures inhibit women from pursuing sex as freely as men do.

It's just that women may often want sex in different ways—and we've been culturally biased against seeing women as sexual beings.

Did you know?

It is a misrepresentation to think that if two people are meant for each other and are in love, sexual relationship should not require work—that, the love and the meaningful relationship, would automatically fire the mood and the arousal.

Everything in the universe eventually demagnetizes when left in proximity to something of the opposite charge. Magnets do, and so do men and women.

Think of sex as the 'oil' in a vehicle and the work put in to get the zing back, as periodical maintenance or accessorizing. Think of sex as the wine bottle in your bar and the experiments/strategies as the decanter to oxygenate the wine to enhance its flavour. Think of sex as the walls and floors in your home and the furnishings, as the change you would typically crave for periodically. A few people reported that just by taking the survey and reflecting on what they felt they could work on, they became more articulate about what they wanted in the marital bed and at the same time became more perceptive in receiving signals from their partners about what they desired.

This is a 'work' that you will enjoy not just while doing it (provided it works for the pleasure of both) but will enhance the bond quotient between the couple long after the work, just like an increased BMR helps you lose weight even at rest!

There are lots of things one can do to get in the mood for sex. Some cited by the therapists are 'a lighter meal', 'fantasizing in advance', that long bath, sexy underwear, etc. Confronting underlying problems in relationships can really help too.

Some think it's wrong to continue masturbating, that it should no longer be necessary, that they are getting all the sex they need.

Counterpoint: Truth is that it is the most common sexual practice the world over, married, with a steady sexual partner or not.

Couples who aren't satisfied with their spouses might

resort to masturbation. But a lot of sexually satisfied married persons continue enjoying sexual pleasure with themselves, which can be highly imaginative and accommodates fantasy and erotica.

A website, Sexual Health and U, describes the myths around masturbation and its effects on marital relationship. It says, 'If one partner masturbates, it does not mean that he or she does not have a desire to engage in sexual activity with the other partner. If anything, masturbation can be seen as reflecting a healthy appetite for sex which is likely to also express itself in desire for sex with the partner.'

Did you know?

Good sex does not include simultaneous orgasms. In fact it can be less stressful and much more rewarding to please each other one at a time.

Managing the paradox

To bond is human. To get bored, tired, frustrated and disillusioned (periodically at least) of that bond is also human. To crave for exclusivity and thus stability with a partner is human. To desire change and get irked with the loss of freedom that this exclusivity demands is also human. To pledge our heart and soul when in throes of love is human but once the euphoria fades and the novelty turns into the mundane, the desire to look afresh for a new high, new excitement, is also human. This paradox of conflicting longings, of meaning one thing with all our heart and then desiring another with all our heart yet again, is sadly very human too.

Understanding the difference between sex, love and intimacy will go a long way to solving relationship problems.

But as a rule couples who talk to one another about sex do better than couples who basically talk to everyone except each other about sex.

4

Fidelity in Chaos

A one-night stand is not an affair. Sure it's an act of infidelity, but it is usually a one-off event. An affair—as I speak of it here—is a more involved relationship, emotionally and physically, and spans a much longer time frame. You have perhaps encountered the expression—the eternal triangle, comprising a married couple and the lover of one of them. The classic affair, however, at least in its initial stages, is conducted in secret—in the absence and assumed ignorance of the third party.

The lure of another

She sat with her face in her hands. How could she have been so selfish and horrible? She knew for a fact that she loved her husband and family to death, yet she had betrayed them all for this 'bad boy'. Both had known that at best it would be a short fling. Yet she had felt helpless then, not simply against his charms but the side in herself he made her revisit. She had been in thrall to the game of flirting: heightened awareness—love songs seemed to have more meaning, sunsets seemed prettier; greater confidence—she was still attractive to a man; the adrenaline flow of excitement—the inherent risks; and the reinvigorated sexuality—the seductive awakening to her newly toned body. But now the secret was out and the game was over!

'It will take me a long time to gain my husband's trust back, to convince him it was just a momentary madness, that the other guy really meant nothing,' she said to her confidante. It was her elder brother fulfilling this role. He knew she meant every word.

'I will never inflict this pain on my husband ever again', she said with determination in her eyes. The brother smiled.

'What is so funny?' she shot at him with angry eyes.

'He may be the first, my little doll, but he is definitely not the last. You will get attracted again... and then again.'

When I met this woman it had already happened again. She told me, 'I struggled with my judgement of how I saw myself—a fallen woman, a nympho! I questioned myself hard; what commitment, shared history, children and family, meant to me. They meant everything, those men nothing! And even as I know that, I also know that my new love interest would not be my last...'

I asked her, 'Why vow monogamy at all?' Why not just make her polyamorous nature known to all concerned? There are open marriages—'don't ask-don't tell marriages'. Why not simply come out in the open from the start?' She looked piercingly at me before continuing, 'Because people change over time. Someone might be polyamorous in their 40s, but not in their 20s, or the other way round.' I nodded.

Why don't women tell their new husbands that they may totally lose interest in sex in ten years? Why do men promise that they will have eyes only for their wives? Because, they mean it then! Because they don't know how they will feel ten, twenty, thirty years down the road—sleeping and waking up next to the same person!

In sharing this anecdote I am not implying that all of us are cheaters, even potentially so. In this world there are all kinds of people—there are those who, having entered into the holy bonds of marriage, are never seriously attracted to another; there are others who, similarly bound by marriage, do get attracted to another but easily control their impulses. In this section on infidelity, my references shall be to those who succumb to their impulses and enter into liaisons outside their respective marriages.

Whilst researching this book I met many people, read numerous case studies (most shared with me by therapists, sexologists, marriage counsellors et al), and perused a large number of blogs and surveys. Some stories stood out—for their stark honesty and deep reflection. To understand what had really happened these people had moved beyond the guilt and the self-disparagement, beyond the damage control mode. They had asked themselves a lot of questions, fundamental ones—the 'how, why and what' of it all. They had understood what was at stake. They were conscious of the societal and cultural conditioning they had been subjected to (and grown up with) which vehemently condemned their infidelity. They had known fully that it was just an affair—with a beginning and an end. One of them quoted a dialogue from a Bollywood blockbuster, *Silsila*: 'After all, *har rishta ek mod per aa kar apni garmi kho deta hai*.'

It was interesting to see some who had had repeated affairs still guilt-ridden and unable to exonerate themselves. They said they had been helpless when 'under the influence'. Then there were my interviews with the spouses of those who had not surrendered to the 'influence,' or the spouses of those who had not had a serious affair. These spouses seemed to have a very simple understanding of their partners. One told me, 'Once a cheater, always a cheater!'

I also had occasion to interview friends and colleagues of exposed philanderers. Some had sympathy for them, some outright condemnation.

It seems to me all of us react to such stories based on our individual perceptions of the issues, based on what resonates with us concurrent with our own knowledge and experience of the persons concerned. Statistics provided by family courts, therapists, detectives, et al, suggest that the predominant cause of divorce today is infidelity. As a thinking person I propose that we move beyond the blind unthinking acceptance of what has been drilled into us by law, religion and society. I propose a deeper questioning of the issue of infidelity—even if there are no solutions.

Whilst there are truths in the perspectives of the various people I have talked of above, I suggest we begin by being truthful about *being human*. Infidelity is surely the biggest challenge to monogamy. To quote Vladimir Nabokov, 'Adultery is a most conventional way to rise above the unconventional.'

The story of an affair is an old one.

Infidelity through time, place and age

Adultery is our inside story, literally. And it is not a new trend.

The *Mahabharata,* our most entertaining and enlightening legacy, has many interesting cases of adultery. If a king is not able to impregnate his queen, the wife is sent for a night-out with a sage (by none other than her mother-in-law). Remember the story of Satyavati who asked sage Vyas, her first (and illegitimate) son, to impregnate her daughters-in-law, Amba and Ambika, so that they could beget heirs for Hastinapur—Dhritarashtra and Pandu.

Kunti used her first boon before marriage and called Surya, the Sun god, who gave her a son—Karna. To hide her transgression of societal laws, Kunti sent off the newborn in a small basket down the river. When Pandu was cursed that he would not survive an act of sex, Kunti used her remaining boons to get sons for herself and her co-queen Madri.

Then there is the ancient story of Satyakam. The most

important identification of brahmins was their gotra, their paternal family tree. When being admitted in a gurukul, it was a so believed that only brahmins deserved to be educated. When the boy (Jabala) requested acceptance as his student, Sage Gautama asked, 'What is your father's name?'

He answered, 'My mother told me to tell you that she is a servant and has served many men in all ways. So she does not know who my father is. Please accept me as Jabala, whose mother is Jabali.' Impressed by his honesty, the sage accepted him and named him Satyakam, a lover of truth.

Lord Krishna, worshipped with his beloved Radha, was someone else's spouse. Stories of amorous activities of Indra and Agni with the wives of some rishis is well known. Our gurus and sages were routinely approached by men to impregnate their wives.

Vatsyayana's *Kamasutra* explains how men can seduce different types of women and the stories are of lovers meeting in secret, hoodwinking the people around them. We have our ancient social custom of niyoga that states that an impotent man's wife can copulate with another man for a child. And we have had kings and noblemen with their harems of concubines and mistresses.

Look at the West and similar instances of adultery and infidelity are to be found—from philandering Greek gods and goddesses of ancient lore to historical personages, and current scandals.

From the past to the present, through latitudes and cultures—traditional Inuits of the Arctic, French sophisticates, isolated tribes in the jungles of Brazil, stern societies of the deserts—infidelity has been documented in every human culture.

Infidelity and us

A wife finds out about her husband's relationship by dialing the number of a woman she has been suspecting her husband to have had an affair with (saved as a business colleague). Another finds out by the whispers from the bathroom in the middle of the night when the husband was chatting with his lover. A husband has his wife's affair revealed when a well-meaning neighbour mentions he saw her take the elevator to the floors with rooms in a local hotel. Another reads a message—'missing you'.

Everyday, Facebook, emails and unlocked cell phones reveal relationships of people we swear could not have had one, couple-friends vacations become the ultimate test of one's limit of endurance, a small business trip with an attractive colleague becomes the fault line on which a marriage of years trips, a single message turns into hopes of feeling alive and attractive!

Everyone, almost everyone, has infidelity stories of someone they knew or know. It is generally accompanied with, ' I cannot reveal the identity but....' It happens to someone out there, till it happens to you (and you are clueless because you thought what you had was 'good'!)

In our survey when we asked, 'How important it was to them for their spouse to be faithful?' or for them to be faithful to their spouse, a whopping 84 per cent said 'important', yet when we asked the same people if they have had an affair, 31 per cent said 'yes'! Most don't intend to have an affair and don't think it will happen to them—but it does. And when it does, you call up your friend requesting them to help you out or be your alibi. And then you become that friend that someone else is quoting!

Even if we're not committing adultery, or being cheated on by a spouse, or speaking about it, we're wrapped up in it somehow. We're caught up in a friend or a family member's affair, covering for them when they're on illicit dates, or picking up the pieces when they're discovered or making the rounds of the divorce courts with them. Or we're obsessing over the public infidelities committed by celebrities and politicians.

And if we are not cheating or thinking about cheating, we take to task the ones who do. We speak of their infidelity again and again, keeping them alive in our active lives; we chastise them, publicize their affairs, and appeal or demand for their ostracism from our noble society. No goodness remains in a cheater, or the goodness can't be trusted—so omnipotent is the transgression in the eyes of the loyals.

Our movies, literature and art, mirror contemporary society—reflecting larger societal trends, issues and conflicts. If we look at the Indian cinema, we have had profound movies that deal with the different causes or effects and aspects of infidelity—boredom, gender inequality, consumerism, betrayal, power struggle, revenge, etc.

From magazines to newspapers, from TV shows to infidelity blogs (where people write candidly about their relationships online—under pseudonyms—and thus share their 'magical' feelings or confessions with the bigger community out there), to 'confession' pages, stories of adulterers tantalize us with the inevitability of their actions. It is sometimes claimed that events in any given story should follow one another in such a way that the trajectory they trace appears to be necessary, so that the listener, reader or viewer is left with a feeling that things had to turn out the way they did, that no other outcome was possible. Most stories on these blogs and confessions have this sense of inevitability, 'I met her after 20 years in a school reunion and…', 'We were a part of a WhatsApp group, I never thought much of him, until he started commenting on each post of mine…' 'I was lonely, it had been a month away from home and…'. From the gym instructor, coach or that salsa or Zumba trainer at the daily exercise, to a colleague, that secretary, the boss or a client at the workplace, to the friend or the friend's husband or the friend's friend at that social evening, to the child's father or mother at a school PTA, to the lone stranger at the bar or at the concert, or at the park, or that friend on a blogging site! Put any two people (not married to each other) in any scenario (work, home, socializing, exercising) and they become the heroes and heroines, even when fallen, who consume us with their narratives of rebellion—so charming compared to our own quotidian and prosaic existence, our 'oh, so moral' lives!

Adultery's omnipresence speaks to us from everywhere. From online sites like the 'Indian Couple Wife Husband cpl-Swapping Sharing Exchanging community' which has more than 21,300 likes to stories of key clubs, wife swapping reported with masala in magazines and tabloids. Did you know there is a group called, 'WhatsApp wife-swapping group' Bhopal'? Similar groups can be found in other Indian cities and towns. Rising infidelity looms in the rising membership of the infidelity-specific dating website for married people like Ashley Madison and Gleeden. Ashley Madison's tagline, 'Life is short, have an affair', has 30 million members across 41 countries. They started operations in India and grossed 65,000 members across Delhi, Mumbai, Kolkata, Bengaluru, Chennai, Hyderabad, and other smaller towns. According to a survey they conducted with their Indian members, 87 per cent of women and 81 per cent of men in arranged marriages claimed to have had affairs. Only 81 per cent of men manage to keep their affairs secret, while nearly all women—92 per cent—have kept theirs hushed up. 76 per cent of married Indian women do not feel it is immoral and 47 per cent of affairs happen on a business trip. For 62.3 per cent men and 51.8 per cent women, the affairs take place at workplace.*

*http://indiatoday.intoday.in/story/religion-of-the-unfaithful-adultery-divorce-marriage-relationship/1/399472.html.
http://specials.indiatoday.com/sexysecrets/infidelity-initiation.shtml
http://indiatoday.intoday.in/story/Secrets+and+lies/1/1662.html

Neeru Kanwar, a psychotherapist, with a PhD in clinical psychology who practises in Delhi, whom I interviewed, said, 'Out of every ten couples who came to me for help with their marriage in the year 2000, four would have come for extramarital affairs. Now, it is seven!' Doctor Kalpana Khatwani, from Mumbai, quoted eight out of ten. Doctor Prashant Bhimani said, 'Where earlier, two to three out of ten women would come to me for cases related to extramarital affairs (their own), today it is six to seven, where earlier it used to be women from the upper class only, now the middle class is showing up at my clinic doors. Whether it is about guilt, or their husbands having found out, or that they want to understand their marriage in the light of the extramarital affair, women are today much more open and bold than when I began my career two decades ago!'

Professor Ahalya from NIMHANS, Bengaluru, said, 'People in our country are very hypocritical in many ways—we like to think of ourselves as very moral in the way we lead our lives and we constantly keep blaming western lifestyle and western values for everything. There are a lot more extramarital relationships that go on in this country than people will ever fully acknowledge.'

'There exists no culture in which adultery is unknown, no cultural device or code that extinguishes philandering'. Helen E. Fisher, author *Anatomy of Love: The Natural History of Monogamy, Adultery, and Divorce* said.

Then why the brouhaha?

We focus so much attention, energy and concern on something so many people flout—with lovers alluringly beautiful and penny plain, gorgeously glamorous and modestly mousy with paramours younger and older. Our attitudes towards marital infidelity have hardened while unfaithfulness has increased. Why?

Officially, we may have switched to monogamy, but unofficially we have always been non-monogamous. When there were no watertight compartments defining exclusivity (specially for men), dalliances were not that threatening or serious—except when, particularly for women, paternity issues were at stake. When 'cheating' was not cheating, there were no cheaters; there were just people who sought 'stuff' outside. History is testimony to how we had exit rules in official monogamy, too, when it was necessary (Niyog, etc., for the continuity of the family lineage). And the non-monogamous male's indiscretions (unless he abandoned his family for the mistress, concubine, lover or prostitute) were excused without much uproar even though it was legally untenable. Patriarchy empowered men to do as they pleased; they could be brazen about it, or they could ensure it was hushed up. Women seeking liaisons within the extended family and affairs with in-laws, visiting tutors and other personnel, even those working within the home, was not uncommon. Of course there was a power imbalance; it was far easier for men to indulge in non-monogamy than it was for women, and the consequences were much harsher for the women. Yet, non-monogamy reigned despite the official monogamy status.

So, what changed?

How and when did relationships outside marriage become synonymous with terms like 'immorality' and 'betrayal'? How and why did it become *personal* rather than something that *people* did? How did it turn into a threat to the family unit and thus the social order, so much so that the state, religion, society, community, etc. had to be pulled in to punish this otherwise accepted transgression? How did something that many did quietly and behind closed doors become so cacophonous? How did its *illegality* take on such a frightful and nasty aftermath? Why did adultery become such a huge misdemeanour when for centuries it was accommodated under some cover or another? How did this become so guilt-ridden and wrong?

Forget the duty-bound state, which must protect the family unit to eventually protect the state; forget the morality-bound religion which must chastise the adulterer to maintain its virtuous standpoint; forget the omnipotent society, which must restrain this impulse to forestall the chaos that it would otherwise bring; forget the spurned spouse—with all her rage, insecurity and humiliation—determined to hurt the betrayer financially, socially and personally.

What is interesting is that the cheaters, too, in most cases, think (especially when caught) that they are wrong, guilty and pathetic to do what they have.

Monogamy is something most people say they believe in and want for themselves; they don't intend to have an affair and don't think it will happen to them—but it does. 'Guilt' is a common word in the lexicon of cheaters, even if they say that they were helpless at the moment. According to a survey reported in *Mid-day*, 'Interestingly, despite having an open mind towards affairs, a whopping per cent men and 86 per cent women feel guilty about having illicit relationships, the dating website revealed!'*

---

*http://www.mid-day.com/articles/65-men-77-women-in-mumbai-dont-

Think about it...

We asked in our survey, 'How did you feel if and when you desired another outside of marriage?' When we gave the option to tick as many as applied to them, 36.78 per cent said that they felt guilty, while 35.63 per cent felt confused. At the same time, 19.54 per cent ticked the 'scared' option, and 47.70 per cent ticked 'excited'!

So again, what changed? Why the guilt and immorality attached to infidelity? Why, in these 'modern times', does the 'wrongness' of it claim so much of our time, energy and resources?

For a long time, we did not have the need—or reason—to treat infidelity as harshly as we do now. Neither did we have the luxury. We lived shorter lives and survival of the family unit meant survival of the individual. Success and meaning of life was drawn from posterity and as a custodian of the next generation rather than in personal and individual sentiments like happiness, growth and pleasure. Besides, the obvious lopsided power equation did not allow one half of the population—women—to create a ruckus about the other half's dalliances. The ones with power could be non-monogamous forcing the ones dependent on them to be faithful (or at least they thought so). Financial dependence meant that women could not afford to annoy their spouses. Women could get away with their romances as long as they kept it hidden from men, or as long as the romances were within the confines of the family, especially when paternity concerns were absent. No contraception meant frequent

---

think-infidelity-is-immoral/15680153#sthash.vqHf5YtS.dpuf

pregnancies and less sexual freedom for women. Confined to their homes, preoccupied with domestic demands, women had few opportunities to meet other men. Mostly, for both men and women, the concept of 'family' reigned over and above the 'individual'. In one sense, they were simpler times, with clear and definite roles for each gender.

What makes being cheated on so threatening?

The breakdown of the joint-family unit and its resultant safety net has perhaps played a role in our exclusivity paranoia.

The currently prevailing psychological dependence on 'the one' is perhaps a major reason for our paranoia with outside intimacies, both sexual and emotional. In earlier times, individuals could rely on a layer of support—from the extended family, from people in their neighbourhood and in surrounding communities; same-sex friendships offered a hedge against loneliness. They filled in with other needs—physical, financial and even sexual—and shouldered the tricky business of filling the gaps that the two left in each other's lives. Some stepped in with attention and advice, some with sympathetic ears and a helping hand. Some played the in-house panchayat and ordered the wrongdoer to get his/her act straight while some counselled the errant black sheep with a softer hand. Essentially, things were *managed* within the extended family unit, and sexual and emotional non-exclusivity did not lead to any major change in the status quo or the relationship of the couple.

Today, we may have specialized systems, complex machines and elaborate aids to go about the business of living but we definitely do not have the web of people that we once had. Where we once shared our day-to-day needs with many others, now we only have a few—even though our Facebook page may boast of a huge number of friends. There are fewer sincere shoulders to cry on even though there is far more specialized advice on Google on how to heal after a trauma or a tragedy. The implication of not having 'the one' is—supposedly—loneliness.

We are not wired to go through the vicissitudes of life alone, we need people we value as physiological and emotional safety nets. The one we have taken our vows with occupies a far more central place in our emotional, physical, psychological and social makeup than they once did. We lean far too much on them for our sense of balance and wholeness than we once did.

And thus, we are faced with a daunting task—to set that bond in cement, make it permanent, impregnable, not just from the outside but from within. We dish out promises by the dozen and lap them up with equal fervour. We do not just commit love and care and togetherness to our partner, we commit love, care and togetherness and *exclusivity*! We do not just commit what we will feel/unfeel for our partner but also what we will feel/unfeel for any third person in an unknowable future. We do not just promise them the exclusively of our bodies, we extract a claim on theirs to the exclusion of all others.

No wonder infidelity sucks so much more now. For we have no support system to help us safeguard the continuity of the relationship from fleeting or deeper infidelities vis-à-vis the larger more substantial future we have chalked out for ourselves with our spouse. 'The one' today can, in the heat of the indiscretion, shortsightedly decide to walk away from the marriage and larger responsibilities, or alternatively, the *one* betrayed can, in a fit of rage, decide to end the unit without really thinking through how relevant the indiscretion really is, even for the betrayer. There are no bumps to halt the tumble.

Marriage therapist Deepak Kashyap says, 'There was constant validation in the past. Think of our social and religious customs, rituals and pujas. In any puja, or auspicious occasion, only the wife could sit alongside the husband. Even if the man had mistresses or girlfriends, in society and family affairs, it was the wife who was honoured and recognized. This kind of ensured that no one is indispensable, a validation of two people still one, whether they felt intimate or not.'

Betrayal, in a world where we draw our sense of worth from 'the one', can seem far more severe, threatening and destabilizing. It is not a promise to an institution or a system as it once was; it is a promise, based on love (with romance and sex as its propeller), which two modern individuals make to each other for a lifetime of togetherness. But—alas! Our dreams, future plans and lives (we live so much longer) outlast our desires.

Earlier, marriages were never really supposed to be contingent on sex and romance; if sparks did fly between the couple, it was just a bonus rather than a foundation, and even when sparks did fly, and inevitably died down, there was an army of support that came into play in the family-system dynamics.

Today, it is not so. Impossible promises are exchanged and there is no support system to help with the gaps and loopholes. Earlier, the unit was bigger than the individual; today, the individual is supreme, and thus, a betrayal of that individuality can make the entire commitment seem suspect.

Perhaps our own malaise has got compounded because of the massive influence of the western world on our own mores and beliefs. A professor I interviewed told me, 'They say "This is my opinion". This individualistic assertion is breaking down the family... You become overly conscious of your individual position... You are actually negotiating with that position in which "I" gains central importance. It has no social base; the society is "us"... Marriage systems break down because of the imbalance between individualism and social aspirations.'

The morality of it all

What made 'cheated on' become so personal, so agonizing and something that erodes sanity?

First and foremost, willy-nilly, we have all become blind believers of the utopian ideal of 'eternal fidelity and romance' as a 'natural' and 'normal' outcome of a marriage based on love—a union of equals. Not for two, five, ten or even twenty years, but till death do us part. The truth is that sexual attraction will wane, romance will cool down, and we will find our partners uninteresting; others will excite and attract us. But when any of this happens we assume it to be symptomatic of a failing marriage. Our society, the media, government agencies, religious leaders—all have this fixated and rigid idea of how our sexual, romantic and family lives should unfold. And if it does not, there is a billion-dollar industry invested in spicing up things for us. We are constantly told how to sex up our lives or bring the romance back or understand the other and to be alert whether our partners are into 'relationships'. We have to do our bit to keep up this perfect eternal relationship!

When any one partner succumbs to another outside, it becomes the failure of that individual and thus becomes extremely personal. Either it is about the cheater who is warped, or it is about the 'victimized' spouse who was perhaps not *good enough*. Either way, it is a personal failure. Because everyone else apparently is not so debauched!

A breaking of vows exchanged so seriously, which others are presumably sticking to, may make our adulterer's other values, too, seem suspect. For how can we trust a person to be a good father/mother, politician, businessman, son/daughter etc. if he/she could not keep such a fundamental promise? And so, it follows that how can we be with a person who cannot be a *good* anything? Infidelity, even though all data from history and sociology show it to be a *human* transgression, becomes a personal and out-of-the-mill one in our lives!

I, me, myself

In this era of growing individualism, where we view self as a self-reliant, assertive, independent entity, endowed with unique dispositions, and when we think of meaning and purpose of life in terms of personal growth, happiness and value, the relationships we form are based less on external obligations and more on the value we find in each other as individuals; values like mutual trust, honesty, uprightness, etc. We form our sense of self, based on such individual values, and hold our loved ones accountable to theirs.

In such a scenario, when our spouse blunders, it somehow becomes about us too, about how we respond to their failing.

Their indiscretion is not just a betrayal of our trust, but our response to it is a reflection of our identity, of the self-image we have projected and believe in. In simple terms, even if we may not want to read so much into the transgression, the individualistic culture we are increasingly aligning with, makes it obligatory for us to take a certain stand. Hillary Clinton faced this dilemma, 'How could she, being the strong autonomous woman she is, live with a cheater?' Someone has to make noise about it! It has to be conveyed that a cuckold or a 'cuckoldess' is less of an individual, and willy-nilly, they must take a stand either way.

Besides, another underlying facet of individualism is that we see faithfulness in attitudes and behaviour from a different angle; rather than being faithful to an institution, it is more about the purity of emotions (love, honesty, etc.) with the person with whom we are entering into a marriage contract. The partners expect and pledge sexual exclusiveness only as long as they regard their relationship as intact and emotionally satisfying.

In this sense, our notion of fidelity is markedly different from those of our parents or grandparents. It is now bound up with feelings. Love and passion may be inextricable—each a sure sign of the other—and yet love can outlast desire. Western independence of lovers has made the barriers of love internal to a relationship. One can never be sure of the love of an independent person. That is why the couple relationship is continuously under internal scrutiny.

Besides, this very individualistic culture encourages the ideals of emotional intensity and spontaneity, of risk-taking and introspection, of exploring change and pursuing it (if what we are doing does not give us a sense of purpose or meaning). And it offers the space and opportunity that comes with this economic and societal independence, to be more 'you' everyday!

And the temptations come alongside too. The excitement of autonomy, the emotional high of owning our desires and expressing them, the power of the pursuit of personal goals, of chasing every iota of the 'I', and then one day, at the command of a certificate (that we ourselves sign willingly) renounce all further sexual and emotional quests and discoveries. We live in the intense pulling of the 'I' in opposite directions—the one saying if you're not passionate all the time, or if you're not feeling in love all the time as the decades pass, there's something wrong with you and the one that reprimands you when you try and do so. In brief, according to the tenets of popular psychology in this new age, feelings and desires must be pursued and expressed; and yet, according to tenets of morality, non-sanctioned desires must be repressed.

The sad fact is that a sexy woman in a bar or a caring man who has been a good listener can excite in us passions long dead or address needs that we can resist only so much!

Think about it...

There is a lot more cacophony now about infidelity simply because there are a lot more people who can now afford to raise hell!

Deepak Kashyap had a unique perspective on our present-day concerns with infidelity (as against it being quite a non-issue earlier). He told me, 'See, it's because of feminism. Instead of giving women the right to sleep with other men, they took away the man's rights to sleep with other women.'

Why does infidelity occur?

We can judge, curse and demean the cheater all we want but it will not help us understand why so many choose to cheat, even though they themselves know it to be grossly wrong and are aware of its enormous negative societal and personal consequences. Most extramarital affairs come with the risk of substantial loss—spouse, children, friendships, reputation, career or position; yet people continue to risk it all for an intimate relationship with an unlikely future. Yes, it is unfair to the betrayed spouse, it stings like hell and plays havoc with their sense of self, it diminishes their standing in society, and it is totally unfair.

But infidelity is too widely and increasingly prevalent for us to be stuck in the blame-game and reprimand mode only. We need to re-examine our attitudes to it, and the way we handle it. It is too complex and commonplace an issue to just simplistically brand the cheater into one slot and the cheated in another. Labels are for convenience but in the matter of infidelity I propose they are counterproductive. We seem to have assumed that individual desires must perforce mirror societal norms and state diktats. Our modern era is undergoing too intensive a social churning for it to be always so. People are thinking deeply about individual freedom and exploring its uncertain limits. When individual desires fail to mirror societal norms and state diktats, we should perhaps ask ourselves: 'Why?'

The biological inclination

Monogamy is not in our DNA. We will desire to be sexually active and the necessary stimuli to desire are absence, anxiety, delay, solitary longing, the very impulses that come to be at complete loggerheads once the marriage matures. However much we may swear adherence to the nobility factor of the monogamous marriage, anything against our DNA is something we're going to struggle with.

That brings us to our fundamental conflict; if we are at heart a moral person—as most of us believe ourselves to be—how do we maintain our own morality and preserve our own integrity in the face of our basic desire to seek diversity, find passion and feel alive?

Helen E. Fisher, a biological anthropologist, asserts that the human brain is naturally designed to seek sex and romance with more than one primary or key partner. This would mean that the brain in true sense allows one to seek and engage in sexual or romantic relations with more than one person simultaneously.

Case study

He went to the counsellor expecting to hear how lowly he had been, how weak, selfish and rotten, and what he could do to make amends. Instead she told him of the conflict between the two deeply-held desires, to be both a loyal husband and a sexual adventurer. He was not unusual; neither in the paradox nor in the hope that shame or remorse would help him stay the course in future or that professional help would eliminate the pull of the opposing wishes. Nor could one be trivialized or labelled.

All of us have struggled with the ebb and flow of this opposing tension over the course of our marriage. The efforts of couples over the ages to cope with that fluctuating tension have provided more than enough examples of adultery to prove that sexual promiscuity is natural, but they have also provided more than enough examples of fidelity to prove that monogamy can be adapted to, as well.

For every four out of ten people who cheat there are six who do not. For every person who at 20 believes in monogamy there is one at 40 who comes to it! Everything is fluid. What is actually natural is the inescapable presence in our lives of conflicting desires. We are monogamists and we are non-monogamists!

We search for love, find him or her, and settle in. Of course our experiences of intimacy and passion, when readily available, are bound to wane in intensity over time, just like our response to any other stimulus.

Texts from an unknown person seem more exciting than the person we've washed socks for or woken up next to for a number of years. The exclusivity factor begins to feel constricting.

'Repeated exposure to a very positive stimulus leads to an increasingly negative emotional response to it.... Complex organisms have a need for variety or novelty; change of stimulus conditions can thus be reinforcing.'*

Think about it...

Extramarital sex and relationships involve a complex pattern of behaviours that include biological influences, psychological factors, social contexts, and the influence of the evolutionary history that has shaped our sexual behaviour. Within each person, the reasons and factors vary—genetics, epigenetics, and conditioning, all play a role.

---

*Donn Byrne and Sarah K. Murnen, *Maintaining Loving Relationshipsin The Psychology of Love,* ed. Robert J. Sternberg and Michael L. Barnes.

There have been questions raised about the most evolutionarily 'natural' kind of human sexual relationship that have existed, and also if they were adapted for long-term or promiscuous form of relationships.

The interesting thing to observe is that humans are adapted for various forms of sexual relationships, both biologically and psychologically. In fact, what has been observed is the presence of 'strategically pluralistic' behaviour where humans adapt to different kinds of long- and short-term relationships based on a variety of factors like one's gender, attractiveness, and also sociocultural and ecological settings. The evolved nature of flexibility has created much diversity across people from different cultures in creating mating strategies. However, now that we are more cultured and moralistic, we not only not choose the mating strategy that suits us best, but feel obliged to pass judgement about the sexual behaviour of others.

The first question we ask when we learn of our partner's affair is 'why'? And we conclude that something must be grossly wrong. Some common explanations:

It's the spouse: That she is a whore and he a lech. That he does not love her anymore, i.e. if he ever did in the first place. That she is not what he thought she was, everything till then about her was a big lie. There can be no future with such a man again—for once a cheater, always a cheater. And the transgression becomes bigger than any shared past, even when it is of decades!

Mindsets: Patriarchal customs assume that when a man screws around it must be because the wife is deficient; feminist theories assure that if a man is fooling around he is an asshole.

Pushed into it: Many a times the cheating partners consciously or subconsciously blame their spouses for creating a situation that 'made them' vulnerable to the affair. The most common reasons cited by men are their partners' disinterest in sex; for women, it's men's emotionally unavailability.

The problem is with the 'cheated on': That you are somehow 'short', not deserving your partner's exclusive love. That, what your partner looked for outside was something that lacked in you.

Even when we may not agree openly with our cheating partners, at some deep level, we will blame their defection to our failings. The instinct to believe the information about ourselves as reflected in our partners' thoughts of us, runs through our deeper consciousness. These hidden subliminal forces explain why the otherwise successful and powerful people are just as vulnerable in their love relationships.

According to Liebowitz, 'This tendency also seems related to the fact that the self-concept of women is, much more than that of men, denned in terms of their relationships with others, and that women feel inadequate when their rival is perceived to surpass them'.

Case study

We were at a friend's place and each of us had had about three to four drinks. Naturally, we all had become a little less inhibited; the mask had started slipping. My husband then put forth a question, 'Tell me, how many times have you felt seriously attracted to another since your marriage?' We were to just give a number; no names were to be revealed. We were four couples in all and as far as my knowledge about the eight of us went back then (our marriages were about seven-eight years old), no one had given in to infidelity. But then, the question was one talking about attraction and not defection. My husband answered first, 'Two'.

I was fairly certain of one of the two, but of the other's identity, I was a little unsure, though I had a name. As would follow, I could not be at rest unless I had zeroed down on the 'other'. I considered the unsure name. Let's call her Anjali. She is gorgeous, fit and classy. I thought of her within the framework of my husband's liking and she seemed to fit! And then, she took on an entirely different persona; cloaked in my husband's fancy, she seemed to me from another world, adorned with grace, power, style and mysticism. To my drunk mind, not even Aishwarya Rai could have paralleled her appeal. Flashes of the future sprang up and I saw myself sitting desolate, watching her in despair in all her grandeur—that I would never be able to match (for starters she was a good eight inches taller than me).

I sidled up to my husband, lifted myself up to his ears despite my high heels and asked in whispers if it was *her*. 'No! Whatever made you think of her?' He was not lying, I could tell.

And in that single moment Anjali and her charms came crashing down. She again became the cool, distant, inefficacious ice maiden that I had always thought her to be and my mind ignored her for the rest of the evening and days till I sat down to write this story…

With the *other, she* came on to him. He was paying too much attention. She caught him in a weak moment. She did not have any morals. He was exploitative. She was a homewrecker.

The suffering needs a buck, the cause of the cheating needs to be arrived at, the blame needs a head and the head must be pinned and hammered!

We see infidelity primarily as a personal problem, a personal failure of the people involved. This is a very simple explanation for a very complex question. Also, in taking the moral high ground, in lashing out at the cheater, in playing the victim game, we may experience a temporary emotional release and are rewarded with the sympathies of the others who ridicule the betraying spouse and the other 'whore' or 'Casanova' as the case may be. But at best, it can only be a facile quick fix and serves only the immediate need of a 'wronged' soul.

How about we take a morally neutral stance that, at least to begin with, enables us to explore the real *meaning* of the affair rather than the ethics of it?

Playing the devil's advocate!

But what if it is not about you at all, *the betrayed*? What if it is about the betrayer?

Sex!

What if it is about the most clichéd reason ever, sex and sexual variety? What if it is as simple as an instinctive craving for novelty in between the sheets? After all, we are humans—a species with millions of years of casual, promiscuous libido flowing through our veins. Over time, marital sex becomes boring; affairs offer a vibrancy and sexual fulfilment is difficult to sustain in a long-term relationship.

'For passion!' a 39-year-old said in an email to the question 'why'. 'For passion! I married young, in my mid-twenties. There was excitement, anxiety and the thrill of my body responding to another that it did not fully know or own. There was passion. But two years into the marriage, settling home, having children, work and a million other nitty-gritties of the quotidian living, left us with no energy, or time for passion. Nor did I miss it. Sex, in marriage, had its own rhythm. A quickie here, a long session there, and at times, I even just lay like a dead log while my husband took care of his business! Somewhere in my mid-thirties the whisperings began, like the seductive call of missing passion. And I could not fit my spouse there! I wanted an unaffected experience, not seduced with the help of props, sexy lingerie, fantasy or watching erotica with the same man I had shared a bathroom with. There is comfort in being able to share a bathroom, but it does not leave much to imagination for the stirrings of passion! I wanted to experience desire that comes from being desired, to once again not know how the body would respond without the preset promptings. I longed for the bliss that comes with an intense sexual awakening. Nothing more.'

Simply put, for many people, an affair can just be about physical gratification or release from arousal or the need for a heightened physical sensation. In this way, sexual desire, in its most objectified form, is a total pursuit of physical pleasure. You surrender to sensations you forgot you could have—a rekindling of the hot buttons that can feel deliciously intoxicating especially when it's been a while that your body has felt electrified in that sense. It's about a whole new sexy way of existing in the world.

According to the relationship experts and marriage therapists I interviewed, a major reason men sought relationship outside of marriage had to do with sex, even if they were getting it at home. It was about the most primitive urge, the 'machismo factor'—expansive and almost uncontrollable sexual appetite. Machismo sexual behaviour is a source of pride for males; by having sex with a variety of women, in addition to their spouses, men demonstrate their expansive sexual appetite. It is a primary way by which they prove their masculinity. These men were generally satisfied with their sexual and emotional life with their wives. Men attributed their extradyadic sexual behaviour more to a need for variety, i.e., a desire for sexual experimentation, sexual excitement, novelty and change, than any other factor. They fooled around because they wanted sexual diversity and the sense of adventure that came with it rather than being unhappy or dissatisfied in their relationships. Like a man in an interview said, 'It was the thrill and the tease that attracted me, we both knew it was nothing more serious'.

A woman I interviewed referred to an affair long over and never discovered. She said, 'I have learned to live without fierce sexual passion though I'm glad for that brief experience to see what it was like'. Another said, 'He didn't want to move into "having sex." It was about time, long, slow, being together. After that, I could step back into my wife role and be happier there too.'

Think of it…

An affair does level the playing field if both spouses have different sex drives.

To feel alive, to relieve boredom!

A line has stayed with me from Patrick Marber's play *Closer*. Anna complains to Alice that, 'They love the way we make them feel but not us'.

There is a certain security in walking back to our lair, opening the door after a full day at work and asking our spouse how their day was or sharing the struggles of our own; yet this very safe sanctuary can simultaneously seem boringly deathlike too, where nothing much 'new' happens. No thrill of the chase, no intrigue of the unknown, no new heart-wrenching secret to be revealed and no baskets to score. Whatever was needed, to be done to win (the heart and the body), has been done. Victory, has been won, our boots have been hung. But every so often, in a Mahesh Bhatt song or a Mehndi Hassan gazal, in the lovestruck faces of a pair of lovers in the park or the adverts of perfumes and chocolates begging to be devoured in passion, in the high-octane romance of the books we read or art we see, we are reminded of our hung boots and our retirement from the thrill of the game of love! The torque of chemistry, the rush of desire, the 24/7 intoxication of a body, mind and soul not yet owned! The waking with their thought, the sleeping in their thought, the songs that had so much more meaning, the flowers that had bloomed for a reason. The delicious pleasure of knowing another as they had slowly unfolded their persons, the joy of sharing our intimate selves, the elation of the endgame, resulting in a classic win-win, the bliss of submitting our body, the ecstasy of holding the other's—we long for that rush when we lived constantly in the land of the *now*! And there was never a lonely moment! There was an ecstasy in waiting too. Like a friend in a relationship said, 'When in a charged relationship, you are always waiting to get up!'

The hung boots stand in stark comparison reminding us of a magical time of a desiring mind and heart, vis-à-vis our present selves buried deep under the anesthesia of deadening familiarity further burdened under a million quotidian mêlées to facilitate the business of living. During the course of researching this book, I asked many interviewees about the major obstacles they faced in their long-term relationships and many cited reasons like betrayal, abuse, indifference, cruelty, etc. Not one said boredom. Yet whenever I mentioned the word their eyebrows would shoot up as if one hidden problem had just came to the forefront. Boredom is like the infamous diabetes, a silent killer working slowly, gnawing away at the relationship.

We go elsewhere, not so much for sex, but because we want to escape who we have become in our tedious routine. We look for parts of ourselves we have let fade in the comforts of our secured relationships. But fortunately or unfortunately, we have two concurrent paradoxical needs, security and adventure; we constantly oscillate between the two—of being bored and dead, or desiring (another) and alive.

What if the longing to feel alive is a million times more compelling than anything else in that particular moment? What if those stray moments of longing cumulate and start fizzing? What if it meant picking one, your own self or the spouse? What if you intuit that your longing is not really for the person you cheated with but for the person you once were—much more *alive* and sparkling? The fun in flirting... The risqué of it all... Those teasing eyes, only meant for the lover, the slight hand brush sending shivers down the soul, and all that goes with it!

A man who had been married for 33 years, and currently

in an extramarital relationship, said, 'In bed she made me feel incredible. Outside the bedroom I felt so admired. I was engaged with life again; my heart was. It fluttered at her messages, those heady long hours on the phone exchanging searching whispered intimacies. I hummed along Arijit Singh's melodies, joined the gym for the six pack and every alternate weekend I found myself in the clothing stores, trying out new styles. I'm not saying it was the right thing to do but, at the time, it felt like the only option. It was like being reinvented.'

How much does morality really stand a chance against the feeling of being reinvented?

According to some therapists, the infidelity index shows many trying to deal with their 'midlife' crisis through a last-chance affair. They've turned 45 or 50, even 60, become grandparents, celebrated thirtieth wedding anniversaries, and it's making them see their youth slipping away. Shinie Antony, author of *Planet Polygamous*, a book about infidelity, says, 'Affairs are open-ended, a fresh slate, power play. Like a new face cream, it's an anti-ageing illusion, playing up a misplaced craving for spontaneity.'

It's chemistry! An alchemy!

We may have selected our life partners diligently based on similar interests or goals and yet we may walk into a party and experience an instant attraction to someone we barely know. Without much conscious thought we find ourselves chatting or talking to them as the warm feeling of mutual pleasantness wades through both of us. A lot of this is biochemistry as some of the most powerful brain circuits for pleasure are triggered. Ever heard of pheromones, the body scents emitted by all of us that influence our attraction subconsciously? Hormonal activity underlies sexual attraction as our noses react to external stimuli and sniff out a flurry of chemicals leading us to potential suitors via a 'subconscious sexual attraction' to certain body odours. Scientists believe that we subconsciously seek out partners with different strengths due to our innate drive to produce strong offspring with greater genetic variability and heightened immune systems.

It can thus be an attraction which we may have less control over!

Sexual chemistry is further fuelled by body chemistry. Regular doses of chemicals such as dopamine and norepinephrine are released (hormones that mimic the effects of cocaine), which promote attraction, resulting in energy boosts, appetite suppression and insomnia. High levels of norepinephrine in the brain increase the experience of joy; dopamine, the feel-good neurochemical, makes us talkative and excitable. Romantics say, 'I am up all night intoxicated, I do not feel hungry'. It is the dope talking. Dopamine, in turn, triggers estrogen and testosterone, due to which the sex drive goes up, and soon enough, willy-nilly one finds oneself obsessing over ending up in the arms of the lover!

You see a new side of yourself in this new relationship

'I had never written poems before, but since she could not accept gifts (for how would she explain them to her husband) I got creative, literally! To be honest I was hearing so many gazals and shayris that poems almost wrote themselves. I remember enjoying the subject while in school, and here I was, twenty-five years down the road, reunited with that interest, through her! It was special to write those couplets and then recite it in person, even over phone. Those were the moments, you know... it was a different thrill, writing those poems...'

You like what the other person brings out in you, skills you did not know you possessed, interests that hadn't seemed compelling, boldness that you did not know you had, lightness that you thought you had left behind when you took to the grown-up role. A lady I interviewed said, 'I would order myself before sleeping: "enough on him, no more thoughts." Or I would decide I would end the relationship for it was too risky, or he was undeserving. But come morning, I would find myself replying to his texts without a second thought, trying to eke an hour out that I had promised would not happen again. There was this sense of compulsion, as if I could not control who I wanted to be anymore. I experienced not only an intensity of emotions but also this anarchy, and I liked how it made me see parts of myself I did not know were there. I liked that I could not manage my emotions.'

It is like you become a new person an imperative lost with your spouse. You sign up for guitar or salsa lessons, you learn to distinguish between different kinds of wines, you hit the gym to work on those flabs, and you like the person that stares back in the mirror. You dress well, work more, take up challenges and ace them to speak of them to your lover. You read books, watch movies different from your interests. And you enjoy this new side of the new you! In one very fundamental way it is like meeting a *new you* who is as attractive to you as the person who has brought about this alchemy. The two fascinate you equally!

An escape into another world, within this world

Aren't affairs living out fantasies? It is a time-out, free of the stressors—(children, in-laws, money, work) that daily life introduces into love relationships. An alternate universe that we dip in just for so long, soothe ourselves and make our way to the everyday real one, having hidden those stars in our eyes.

Let's call the lady I interviewed Shreya. 'Every time I would go on a vacation with my family and saw a shoe that would have fitted him, or a pipe I knew he would have liked to own, I visualized him having it. And then, on my flight home, I would count hours—an hour closer to being in "our city". I was coming home to someone who was waiting! I had to steal those minutes to exchange a quick hi over the phone or whisper how much we missed each other. There was this delicious feeling of being wanted and missed, of being told over and over again how beautiful I was. This secret fantasy world that I could visit—for a moment, a minute or an hour, with or without the lover—was my little dollhouse game. And I liked this new secret world. We were explorers, each with a new best friend. I could tell him stories from my childhood, stories new to his ears, stories of my present times, my likes and dislikes, fears and phobias, my guilt and trepidations. And he heard with so much attention… Like, I said this was a beautiful dollhouse game, which after I had played for a while, I wrapped up and was happy to go back to the real one. The two worlds worked so well from a practical standpoint even though I knew I could not justify it morally. Only if my husband knew that a part of my patience comes from the fact that I have someone to talk to in the afternoon!'

In a long-term relationship, we become frozen in our role, caught in a repetitive loop. An affair offers a clean slate and a refreshing unpredictability, a newness. We are often pleased, surprised, relieved or thrilled, to find that in this affair we show up as very different from the person we are in the marriage. We are funnier, sexier, smarter, more compassionate, wiser, kinder, more wonderful, fulfilling and pleasing—even to ourselves! After all, it is for an hour or two, sometimes a stray weekend here and there. It is easy to maintain the illusions, even of oneself.

Romance is a breeze when carried out in secret, fleeting meetings with little time for real life to intrude. And it is a space where we have not even shared the full real 'I'. You have put your best foot forward and so has the other. It is Stage One of romance and it is nothing short of perfect! It's a new you wrapped in desiring and being desired, attracted and being attractive. You are treated as special. You are heard, understood, appreciated and wanted. It is a confidence-builder. You feel validated in a different sense. In this secret world, you are perfect, the lover is perfect, and the world is perfect! What a capsule of goodies! Your own secret perfect world. A world that does not involve responsibilities, expectations, EMIs, bills, children, housekeeping or rules. The high art of philandering is finding ways to steal perfect little moments. You know that what you're doing is wrong, but it feels so right. It's your secret, and it's exciting.

In this world of cyber affairs that we live in, it is far easier to carve out this secret perfect world. The two augment each other—the need for fantasy and the virtual world. With thousands wanting and waiting a click short on their desks, whether at home or work, whether travelling or waiting at the lounges, the laying down of the bedding can be sinfully effortless.

It can be an escape...

When some people have affairs, they're not intending to leave their spouse. It's more a situation of their running away from a problem. They see the other as an opportunity to escape from reality. A man I interviewed said that an affair for him was an escape from the dark reality of his failing business and amassing depression. At work, it was the balance sheet and phone calls of debtors, and at home it was watching his young son about to finish high school and have no family business to fall back upon. In his lover's embrace, he felt absolved of all his worries, and much more like he had once been...

Simple and pure happiness!

I remember Prasanna aunty from 25 years back. Prasanna aunty was obviously the happiest of the lot. She did not haggle with the vendors, did not participate in the marathon bitching sessions whenever the womenfolk got together, she did not keep account of 'who-invited-whom'—especially to a party she was not invited to. The trivial preoccupations of the other aunties seemed to bore her. For my 15-year-old self, she was an enigma.

I sensed uncle (her husband) had nothing to do with her being different from the others. He was exactly like the other uncles—took her for granted and ordered her about. Our families had holidayed together and I thought him generous but quite unromantic, quite like the others.

Then, one chilly evening in Kullu, I overheard a hushed gossip session in which she happened to be the subject. Prasanna aunty had a lover back home—her nandoi (sister-in-law's husband). I detected envy in the tones and manner of some of the women. The suggestion was made and immediately accepted that her sunny persona was the result of her blissful state of affairs—a generous husband and a passionate lover on the side!

Affairs, with the attention and the goodies they bring (if and till they are discovered), do make us undeniably happy. And it is easy to be good when happy. We do not grudge others their place in the sun, are less crabby and jealous. We become far more tolerant and less judgemental.

And then...

Affairs fill the craving for drama, risk and excitement. And it is a rebellion against a system. It is, after all, eating the forbidden fruit!

Affairs fulfil your curiosity. To see the 'how'. How would sex be with another? How would your body respond? Does the libido go up? Does your body find him wanting?

You are never lonely. Formulating texts, receiving them, checking mails, phone calls, planning a rendezvous, thinking about the rendezvous, preparing for it. And when nothing else, you are daydreaming about the beloved. You are really never lonely!

And then it is about communication. You have someone willing to share the minutiae of your life, your otherwise humdrum existence.

And it can be about the delightful knowledge that you still have the capacity to seduce.

In the face of tragedy, illness, or loss, affairs can provide a shot of adrenaline that helps recapture one's lost vitality.

Ultimately, it is not the sex that glues the adulterous relationship together but the talk about sex and the power it has to transform our idea of ourselves.

A lady I interviewed sent this over email.

Top reasons to have an affair with a married man:

1. They are always starved for sex and give you all you want.
2. You are the most important date on their calendar.
3. They are probably not doing it with anyone else.
4. They'll tell you it's the best *** they've ever had in their life and honestly mean it.
5. They will tell you things they have never told anyone else and actually listen when you do the same.
6. They will make you feel like the most desired woman in the world.
7. They won't leave you for another woman, because you're probably her.
8. When you find another boyfriend, they have to take it quietly.
9. You never lose your independence.

Another interviewee told me her husband was a really nice person, even if predictable and habit-bound, and she felt telling him of her affair would be cruel.

A marriage therapist I interviewed told me that the hurt partner usually wants to go into 'why him? Why her?' For them it is about the *other*, and thus, in one sense, about themselves—'what did she have that I did not?' An affair of the spouse becomes about the victim. While there may be some substance in it, it can't possibly be all. The marriage therapist encourages couples to go beyond the whole 'victim-betrayal' prism to understand what it was that their spouse liked about themselves in the affair.

How was he or she different in it? A lot can be gained by going beyond the repeated loop of 'I discovered your affair-am terribly hurt—you must be awfully guilty-make penance—we start afresh all over again and you must never betray me again.'

It is about seeing the spouse as an individual with his own complex cultural, social, financial and psychological makeup, rather than a person who is first our husband or wife, is to see the affair in the larger context of multifaceted life rather than a narrow linear frame. Also, there is peace in knowing that you did not cause your spouse to have an affair. There are many layered forces at play rather than just the 'moral' standpoint of it. In the end, whatever we may choose to do or not do can only be one part of our multidimensional history.

Think about it…

Is it possible that an affair is perhaps not always a symptom of problems in the marriage?

Is it possible that, the primary motivation for the affair was not to deceive or betray the spouse?

Is it possible that in part at least, it was about human yearnings—yearnings that inevitably stand at loggerheads in societies propagating a stern monogamy.

Our struggles with love and desire are a fundamental part of our human condition.

Locating the affair in the context of marriage

I meet her every year at the Jaipur Literature Festival—tall, slim, self-assured and very American. She comes to India to buy semiprecious stones and plans her visits on the festival dates. In one of the events we were seated next to each other and began speaking about love and infidelity in long-term relationships. Her story was heart-wrenching and one many of us would identify with. Eleven years into her marriage, she had an affair with a colleague at work. The affair was discovered within a year and, when confronted by her husband, she decided to walk out of the marriage with her 8-year-old daughter because, 'they were in love and it seemed the right thing to do'. Her affair partner, too, left his family and they moved in together. By the time her divorce came through the relationship was on its last leg. She said, 'At first, the sex was fantastic. I hadn't felt so alive in years. When with him, everything was *stronger*; flowers seemed to bloom for us, the clouds rumbled to prompt an unscheduled rendezvous. I felt high all the time and had so much energy. I thought I was in love.'

But all that fizzled out rapidly as they began sharing their everyday life and with it the quotidian squabbles. Besides, the guilt of her affair partner and some amount of social ostracism took the exhilaration off the nice moments and made the bad ones worse. Very soon, the affair partner confessed that he had made a mistake and was back with his wife, leaving our tall American beauty, a single working mom and now an unhappy lonely woman.

When she shared her story with me nine years had passed. 'After he went back to his wife, I tried to work it out alone for a while. You can call it ego. By then my husband had moved on. I have been in a few relationships since; some serious, some fleeting, but none have been for the long haul. Today, I wake up alone and sleep alone. My affair partner is back with his family and content. I am alone because I chose something that looked and felt so similar to love in its limited, furtive framework but collapsed very soon after it set foot on real grounds. Alone is not a nice space to be in. I share this story for all others to think hard before they make any life-changing decisions thinking it to be *love*. Only if I knew then what I know now, that the lover was meant to be exactly that—a lover.'

It is easy to confuse the euphoria of being attracted and attractive, of lust and its satiation, and the charming feeling of being appreciated, with love. To experience novelty, after years of predictability that marriage inevitably tends to be, makes us irrationally shortsighted. The rush of novelty and the hormones that are released play further havoc with our sensibilities. It feels a lot like love. Besides, we do not have a model in which we can make space for these natural cravings of lust, the rush of the chase or being chased or the enchanting feeling of being wanted. Covering it up in the garb of love lends, at least to some degree, a sense of justification and respect. Otherwise we are just pigs or sluts.

Ironically, the very culture that tries to control infidelity by denigrating it as immoral, ends up making the cheating partners read more into their affairs than perhaps they should. In betraying the spouse there is a lot at stake. If one is willing to risk having an affair even then, perhaps it is really love, perhaps it is the soulmate we really deserve! The very strictures against having an affair endow it with a thrill and a romance that is hugely enticing. The husband with his smelly socks and unbecoming burps—or the wife with her constant nagging and criticism—

seem poor foils for the charms of the lover.

There's the old adage—men give love to get sex and women give sex to get love. Gender gap in behaviour may have decreased, yet the idea of love can be an easy and powerful medium to fulfil our deep-seated individual needs. A man in an affair may promise love that he does not really feel; the woman in that affair may accept that professed love even when she may suspect it because she does not have the space to really question it. A woman bathed in the bliss of feeling desired and wanted, convinces herself it *is* love, so strong is her need to feel noticed or validated.

Dr Dorothy from VIMHANS says, 'Sometimes there is no reason, sometimes it is just a new passion. It's just something new and very attractive—it has nothing to do with love or marriage. The cheating partner doesn't feel the need to justify. But the spouse wants a reason, s/he will not accept an answer like, "I don't know." It is emotionally distressing for the spouse to take a "big" betrayal like infidelity without an equally colossal reason. There has to be a why. So then the cheating partners tend to give reasons, and love is a convenient, perhaps the most easy, one.'

Did you know?

Following is the survey that we conducted on Monkey Survey:

'If and when you were attracted to someone else, did you feel...' 30.61 per cent ticked on 'they thought something was wrong with them' while 10.20 per cent felt that something was wrong with their partner. A whopping 30.61 per cent felt that something was wrong with their marriage, while 39.46 per cent felt that something was wrong with the institution of marriage itself.

And then, at some point in an extramarital affair, the partner says, 'There must be something wrong with your marriage or you wouldn't be involved with me.'

And if it is love, then we may start questioning our attachment to the marriage itself! Whoa! One could stop here, take a step back and ask some hard questions both about the self and the cheating spouse when in an affair. Not grand questions, but very simple ones.

Do you know them enough to love them? Do you know their anger triggers and weaknesses? Do you know their vulnerabilities and irrationalities? Have you seen them without their masks? Have they seen you without yours? There is a saying that you cannot really know someone unless you have lived with him or her.

Does passion/desire mean love? Is it perhaps you love how they make you feel? And you feel you MUST have that person in order to have that experience? Are you confusing the pleasure in the affair as love for your affair partner? What if the intense feelings aren't necessarily for that other person so much as it is for the fact that you've been reunited with a long repressed part of yourself? Like this lady said in an interview, 'It is ridiculously unfair to compare a long-term relationship with a romance still in Stage One.'

Do you want to hang around after the rendezvous? Talk about stuff that is boring but an essential fibre of life? Discussing issues of children, work, health etc.? Once you have felt satiated do you itch to return to real life?

Has the novelty faded? When you have been there, done that, pursuing and pursuit are not as charming. How is the affair then? This is typically when many women complain of not being able to handle the guilt and men change their lines from, 'My wife does not understand me' to, 'I think it is unfair to her'.

A lady I interviewed said to me, 'It is amazing how something that made me feel so incredible when it started, can now make me feel so terrible!' A man in an email said, 'She had become demanding. It had turned tedious.'

Look around. How many affairs have led to marriage? How many have fizzled out and lost steam? Why? Did the love disappear? Try and read between their lines...

How many of those extramarital affairs-turned-to-marriage have worked out?

Spoiler alert: the statistics are dismal.

In the same vein, let's give the cheating spouses the same benefit of doubt. That they think it is love and got swept off their feet. And will land back soon. Like another woman who wrote about her husband's 18-month affair with his secretary: 'He thought he'd fallen in love; he probably did, for a while.'

Affairs seldom last more than a few months. After it's over we realize what it really was and why we went into it. The realization however comes much faster if the affair comes out in the open and the cheating partner leaves the marriage for the affair. With the passage of time and the hours spent together, the little irritations compound and the romance diminishes. From Stage One—of idealizing, we have moved to stage two—of disillusionment.

Noel Biderman, the CEO of Ashley Madison (a website where married people come to seek affair partners) was asked about the typical life cycle of an affair. His response was 'Between one to three months'. In our country, given our greater social antipathy to affairs, there is much more shrouding of it in secrecy; consequently, affairs might enjoy a longer lease than projected by Mr. Biderman.

This puts it succinctly:

> Love is a temporary madness, it erupts like volcanoes and then subsides. And when it subsides, you have to make a decision. You have to work out whether your roots have so entwined together that it is inconceivable that you should ever part. Because this is what love is. Love is not breathlessness, it is not excitement, it is not the promulgation of promises of eternal passion, it is not the desire to mate every second minute of the day, it is not lying awake at night imagining that he is kissing every cranny of your body. No, don't blush, I am telling you some truths. That is just being 'in love', which any fool can do. Love itself is what is left over when being in love has burned away, and this is both an art and a fortunate accident.
>
> —Louis de Bernières, *Captain Corelli's Mandolin*

Think about it...

Does monogamy prove love? Does infidelity prove the lack of love?

According to Dr Helen Fisher, of Rutgers University in New Jersey, there are three very distinct paths in the brain for relationships—sex drive, romance and attachment. The three factors work together and also independent of each other.

Dr Fisher explains, 'You can feel deep attachment for a long-term spouse, while you feel romantic love for someone else, and you may feel the sex drive in situations unrelated to either partner. In fact, you can lie in bed at night and swing from deep feelings of attachment for one person to deep feelings of romantic love for somebody else.'*

What makes romantic involvement or idealization such a problematic state is its ability to flow in many ways at once. It is not uncommon for individuals to be, at least in the short run, out of sync with each other.

The chakra-relationship scale

The theory of chakras is an ancient science and one that enjoys a high place in the yogic and meditative kriyas. Chakras are energy centres, located along the spine, through which our prana or the psychic energy flows. Each of the seven chakras is associated with a certain body part and organ. Based on that, each chakra corresponds to a specific aspect of human behaviour and development. Thus, it is important to understand what each chakra represents, how to open the centres, and keep them in a harmonious sync with one another.

I have been practising chakra dhyana regularly and I am deeply committed to the practice. Chakra dhyana, meditating on these energy centres, is a kind of communication, much nuanced and needed, helping us understand the deeper layers of our thoughts and actions. Chakra dhyana helps in building

*http://www.ted.com/talks/helen_fisher_tells_us_why_we_love_cheat/transcript?language=en

the relationship with one's own self, starting from the physical and the sexual, to the emotional and the psychological, to the intellectual, and culminating in the spiritual. It is an intense conversation with self. I have learnt over the past years that this subtle energy powerhouse and its functioning has significant bearings on my attitude, behaviour and actions. I realized how the relationship with these inner chakras can be used as a measuring tool to understand my own mind-body-soul connection to another outside of it. I invite you to measure the significant 'other(s)' in your life via this tool. It may help you gain a perspective that we are normally blind to, while under the spell of a thrilling new interest in our life!

Mūlādhāra: The base or the mool chakra is located at the perineum, the base of spine. It is the chakra signifying the earth element and gives us the quality of cohesive resistance and weight or solidness. Patience and greed are the attributes of this element, survival its desire. It deals with self-preservation and tasks relating to the physical and basic needs like food, shelter water and safety. It is perhaps related to our two carnal instincts (that is driven by the needs of the body, as opposed to the higher functions of the mind)—food and sex.

To me, this chakra means base physical desire; the natural instinct to satisfy what the carnal body craves for. Perhaps this has its genesis in evolutionary biology—to mate with as many as possible.

At this point, check:

Think of the lover that you are involved with. Is the relationship at the Mūlādhāra? Is it about the curiosity of what a new body will feel like, about 'getting' him or her, scoring another number (sounds very close to the survival instinct doesn't it)? Also if it is your spouse involved in an extramarital relationship, for once, separate yourself from the hurt of it and think dispassionately about the attraction that your spouse feels towards a woman he looks at with lust. Is it just about this base primal instinct? If so, what is born in the body will become irrelevant as soon as it finds satiation.

Svadishtan—or the Sacral Chakra lies about three centimetres above the Mūlādhāra Chakra, also in the genital area between the coccyx and the sacrum. This signifies the water element and is experienced as fluidity. This sacral centre is connected with the fluid functions of the system, like the semen and urine. This chakra thus represents desire, pleasure, sexuality, procreation, fantasy and creativity.

To me, this chakra means the eroticization of sex. It is not just an act of release from arousal via orgasm but a deeper experience that distinguishes us from animal-like mating. It involves feelings with perhaps a more equalizing equation between the two in the act. It is being sensitive to giving as well as receiving; we may know it as lovemaking. We can have sex at will, but lovemaking is a gift that comes and goes of its own accord. And this gift as we see comes rather easily during the romance stage in a relationship. Though it may involve feelings, essentially, it is about the passion in sex and thus about the 'body'. With the passage of time, though, it may lead to a deeper relationship.

At this point, check:

Think of your relationship with the lover. Is it about passion? The slow knowing of another's body, the rhythmic sync with this new 'other'? Is it the craving for the sensual? Is it about the complete involvement of all the senses at that time and because of feeling 'whole' temporarily? This sense of 'wholeness' in pleasure may seem very much like love!

Think of your cheating spouse. Is it this passion with a new body that you are assuming to be his love for another?

The Manipur chakra occupies the upper abdomen and is concerned with the digestive system, muscles, pancreas and glands... Manipur is about action, doing, and breaking inertia.

To me it is about moving from kaama to the essential khana, the everyday living and our duties regarding others who are dependent upon us for their survival, essentially our dharma. This happens when the relationship is in that sense at an 'everyday' level, where the two are connected, that an everyday interaction is necessary—in essence a relationship which is connected through the stomach and so is 'everyday' in nature. This is when two join forces to make a life together. The relationship to me then is in the Manipur zone. Also another part of being everyday is when you share joy and laughter, anger and vulnerabilities, when you can be depended upon and offer such dependency to your spouse or partner.

At this point, check:

Think of your relationship with your lover. Is it as real as everyday living, or is it about the dreamlike fleeting moments snatched occasionally? Do you share your weaknesses and celebrate your strengths? One easy test could be when you think of a big moment in your life, either a victory or a crushing loss, who do you think about sharing it first with? With your lover?

Think also of your cheating spouse in this context; where is s/he in this 'everyday' sense with his/her lover!

Anahata or the heart chakra is located in the region of the heart. This chakra is situated in the centre of the seven chakras, with three below the world of matter and three above—the world of spirit. This signifies the air element within us. It occupies the heart region and is associated with lungs, heart, arms, hands, and the thymus gland. We fall in love through our heart chakra; it is the centre of love, compassion, harmony and peace. Here, 'I need' becomes 'I love.' Love shows us that the happiness of the other is our happiness and that giving is like receiving, or even better. It is about the ability to have self-control and to accept the self and the others. This chakra is the house of the soul. The two triangles inside it symbolize the union of Shiva and Shakti. Remember the lines, 'Love itself is what is left over when being in love has burned away'.

To me, to be in this zone with another can only happen when we are no more driven by our selfish needs of the other, when we need them because they fulfil a certain thing for or in us. This is when we move beyond the otherwise compulsive urge to own or contain, to limit or to possess, to use or to trade. This is when all mathematics flies out of the window. It is when we rise beyond our need of that person and think of her/him as a whole and not just an appendage of our needs.

At this point, check:

Think about your lover. Have you reached the Anahata zone with him or her? Are you at least moving in some sense towards this kind of an unconditional space? Is your cheating spouse in the Anahata zone with her/his lover?

Vishuddhi chakra is the energy centre in the throat region and is located at the base of the throat. It presides over the ears, nose, throat, neck and tongue. It is the chakra of truthful communication and expression. There is this little story associated with the Vishuddhi. For a thousand years, the gods and the Asuras churned the ocean of milk while Vāsuki, the serpent, spat venom from his hundred heads. Lord Shiva drank the poison during the samdudra manthan. His throat turned blue, but the world was saved. Vishuddhi in particular means to purify or to clean. Purification not only occurs on the physical level, but on the level of the psyche and the mind. All problems and unpleasant experiences that we have 'swallowed' and suppressed during the course of our life continue to exist in the subconscious mind and it is in this zone that they have to be faced and resolved with wisdom.

To me, throat chakra is another step deeper on the relationship plane. It is when the two drink each other's poison, in the sense that the two see each at their worst, with all their weaknesses and meanness and cruelty, and be with them still! It is acceptance. And it is here that the two help purify and cleanse each other through their relationship. We can also see this is as supporting the other in his or her growth, helping them deal with their deep-seated issues. It is about having the trust to open up our vulnerabilities and having the faith that the vulnerabilities will not be used against us.

At this point, check:

Think of your extra-dyadic partner vis-à-vis this aspect. Do you have the faith to open yourself emotionally to your lover? To let him see you at your worst, to let him witness the poison within? Do you have that faith? Have you seen his worst? Having seen that poison, do the two of you still want to stick around? Not because you have to, but because seeing someone at their worst, is at some level a *more* profound connection? Also, love at this stage can be more than just accepting, it can be about helping the other deal with his poison, in any which way we can. Ask yourself, are you helping your partner grow? Is he/she?

Here I am not referring to the natural state of newness and expansion that comes, at least initially, when a new love enters our life with his/her new world. I am referring to a much deeper faith that comes after all the firsts have been done with and the relationship is at a stage where we cannot but reveal the not-so-pleasant parts of our personality at a much more open and intimate level. Do we then become, at least in parts, an agent to help the other cleanse? Think of your cheating spouse. Is his/her relationship with the extra-dyadic partner anywhere close to the Vishuddhi? Or are they still at their best behaviour with each other?

Ajna or the Agnya chakra is the chakra of the mind and is located between the eyebrows. It is also called the trikuti, or third eye. Ajna is the seat of the higher intelligence and governs the higher mind, will, and conception. Intuitional knowledge is obtained through this chakra. There is no observed and no observer. All dualities cease.

To me, to be at the Ajna in a relationship is to be both yin and yang to each other and with each other. To complement as and when needed, to operate from this space of 'whole'. The desire is for the complete union. This is the stage when one is not superior to the other but where the two complete each other not just physically and emotionally but in their minds too. This is a truly equal state. Normally, it is the inequality that keeps the relationship smooth but to be in the Ajna means to be complete with each other because you are complete in yourself. The play of ego then is just a silly game that two play with each other when they are bored—for in their minds they do understand this omnipresent sense of equality.

At this point, check:

Think of your relationship with the lover. Do you connect at that level? Have you, even for a few moments, found that sync? Think of the Ajna regarding the lover of your spouse. Is it in that sense egoless and complete?

Sahasrara is located at the crown of the head beneath the Fontanelle. This area is called the Brahmarandhra, or the ' door to Brahma.' In essence, Ātmā, the self, and Paramātmā, the supreme self or the divine consciousness, both reside within us but the Paramātmā is not accessible to us due to the 'I' that we carry with us everywhere. Moksha here means union of the Ātmā with the Paramātmā, or of the individual with the universe, the highest experience possible for a human life. This is when one reaches Samadhi, the pure bliss of total inactivity.

To be in Sahasrara in the relationship is to be in the state of universal brotherhood. No 'I', no 'you', and no 'other' exists. Although this final stage is easier to talk about than to be in, it won't harm us to at least imagine what this state would mean vis-à-vis man-woman relationships. Universal brotherhood would ensure that there is no jealousy whatsoever as there is no wish to claim the other as 'mine', or insecurity. This in no way implies that the attraction between male and female might wither. Only the bulky baggage of concepts and belief systems that we carry along will get dropped, leading to acceptance of whatever *is*.

Think about it...

Making love with a woman and sleeping with a woman are two separate passions, not merely different but opposite. Love does not make itself felt in the desire for copulation—a desire that can extend to an infinite number of women—but in the desire for shared sleep; a desire limited to one woman.

Accident-prone zones in marriage

Situational?

According to many therapists, first affairs for men begin while their wives are pregnant or lactating and sex is put firmly on the back-burner. Finding the wife preoccupied with the newborn, some husbands feel unloved and unnoticed, and plunge into affairs. Others find their wives' changing bodies a turn-off and seek sex elsewhere.

Another situational trigger could be an undesirable change leading to trauma or stress. It could be the death of a parent or a close friend or the empty nest state, or it could be a huge setback in business or career or any other situation which may put undue pressure on one or both.

It can also be as everyday as loneliness. A single lady I interviewed said, 'During the long summer vacations when the wives are away at their parent's homes or perhaps vacationing, the men in the neighbourhood call, on some pretext or another.

"I was in the area and thought would drop a hello." "Do you want to meet up for coffee?" "Some table tennis?" All harmless. Summers end and the calls stop.'

A crisis of faith in oneself or a significant other can be another trigger. One person in the marriage may try to gain a sense of power through an affair.

Another situation could be just a one-off slip up as an opportunity presents itself. It can be with someone you have been flirting with for a while, or after that extra glass of alcohol, or after a bad day at work.

Sometimes the affairs can be motivated by one's need for revenge! It is the retaliatory affair. It can be about deep-seated resentment because of unhappiness in the marriage, it could be the affair of the marriage partner. Affairs motivated by revenge are generally short-lived.

Think about it...

I am not trying to excuse these but trying to understand an affair in the context of a situation. Relationships borne out of a situation (crisis) will die when the situation changes. Wouldn't it?

To be noticed?

'My husband', an interviewee said, 'was actually a better lover than the two men I have had an affair with, but when I am with my lover, he is totally focused on me. For those moments I am his goddess! I tried to speak to my husband about it. Nothing changed.' Another said, 'I was watching my marriage video and cried as I remembered my vidai. I took his hand gently in mine. He squeezed it for a second before going back to his emails. I went to my room and opened Facebook and accepted my college crush's friend invite.'

Psychologist Deepak Kashyap said, 'The most common problem in any marriage or we can call it in human life for that matter is, "I do not feel important. I do not mean anything. Or I have stopped to mean something to that person who said I mean so much." This is symptomatically represented in different ways in different couples. For example, "He does not call me enough" to "He does not send me gifts enough' to "He is more interested in other people' to "He is sleeping with someone else'. Any sign or symptom that tells us we am dispensable, we are not important or we do not mean enough gives us sadness, anxiety and anger (depending on our personality) in marriage and in life'.

My numerous interactions with therapists confirm that as marriages mature and relationships cool down, as they are likely to, many people seek out relationships outside the marriage. In the beginning, it is camaraderie, friendship, a sharing of confidences, with no thought of physical intimacy; then over time, lines blur, intimacies mount. One compliments the other on personal things—a new hairstyle, a matter of dressing. It could be an accidental brush of bodies, it could be shared likes. The progression from emotional attachment to romantic and then sexual relations can be so smooth and gradual, appearing to one's conscious mind as an enigma, or perhaps an accident. How many of us have heard the line, 'I don't know what happened but it was just supposed to be an innocent coffee.' Perhaps we, too, have not appreciated the unobtrusive yet inexorable onset of infatuation, thinking our mature selves can handle the thrall of temptation. Unmet needs finding fulfilment in another can be quite reactive!

Online friendships, too, follow the same pattern. They slowly turn into more and often people do not realize how far things have gone until sex comes into play. These people truly can't explain how the affair happened, since they never meant for it to.

Think about it...

It is nice to be in love when you get married, but the 'in-loveness' in marriages comes and goes whilst the issues stay. So long as the others 'outside' are adding, and not substituting, the core requirements that must come from the primary relationship, it is fine. But the fundamental moving away of partners begin, when, instead of roping in their marriage partners in their essential unmet needs, they realize them with another. It is a matter of time before the emotional needs start merging with the physical.

Substituting?

Affairs complement marriage with romance, passion and sexuality. Some use dalliances to consciously substitute what they are not getting in the marriage. It is their way of meliorating their marriages by satisfying some of their needs outside the home. One man wrote in an interview, 'She accuses me of being a sex addict. I miss the closeness as well as the sex. I see my lover once a week. It may not be right but at least my marriage is better for it because I'm not hounding my other half.' Another woman interviewee wrote, 'I am not looking for a soulmate, just to be appreciated and adored. My husband irritates me, like all my long-married friends are irritated by their husbands. He leaves the loo seat up, burps and snores. He is not romantic, does not compliment me on my dresses or slides his hand up my back without wanting sex in return. My EMAs help me tolerate all that. I love the flattery, the flirtations.' Another said, 'I have no desire to end my marriage. Instead I am just looking for some excitement in an otherwise dull routine.' Another said, 'As great as the sex is with my lover, we really do not have much to say to each other.'

One theory is that you have an affair because you do not want to break your marriage over something like lack of sex, want of attention, or minor irritants.

Testing?

For some, an affair is just a testing ground, a foil, for gauging their spousal relations. Somewhat like we test our blood pressure or sugar levels! Like an interviewee said, 'I would have never known how much I loved Karan if I had been faithful to him.'

At times one gives scant thought to why one would like to preserve the marriage. Then, if perchance a situation arises when the affair could stand exposed, one is forced to face the reality of facing the spouse's reaction—perhaps even a break-up of the marriage. Many realize only then what the marriage means to them, that they would like to preserve it, and conclude it is the affair which must end.

Sometimes an affair is a cry for attention, like a wake up call that says, 'Let's pay attention to what we have built here.' It forces the couple to take stock, unearth festering fundamental issues and address them despite where it may lead. In one significant way an affair does shake the marriage from its routine, pushed-to-the-background, deadening stupor. An affair spurs both the cheating and the cheated-on partner to confront what is the least they want from each other.

It is a choice made voluntarily yet again, by the straying partner. Aloud it says, 'I choose'. The tacit understanding is, 'It is has been ten, twenty, thirty years to our marriage and yes I choose you once again to the exclusion of the other that you are so threatened by'.

It is avowing fresh commitment to the union. It is pencilling-in yet again the boundary line. It is a fresh declaration towards exclusivity. Coupledom is a sustained resistance to the intrusion of third parties. But the couple needs the third party to have something to resist and thus say once again, 'What we have is something special'. We need our rivals to tell us where we are with our spouses! Two's company, but three makes the couple a couple!

Jealousy sustains desire or at least rekindles it. A lady interviewee said, 'As he paid attention to the busty woman in the party, and she matched his flirtation, I was mad at them both. But once home, I felt this ravenous hunger for my husband!' The suspicion-ridden marriage bed can be a pretty steamy place. Because the certainty and the taken-for-grantedness is gone!

Autonomy?

Marriage is a shared duality. But it is also about doing things as a unit. Often, we speak individually but use the 'we' to denote the couple together as a unit. Likewise, when others address us using 'you', they often mean not just the individual spoken to but the couple taken together. Marriage leaves little scope, whether in theory or in practice, for an autonomous self.

Considered in the light of this perspective an affair can seem a powerful assertion of individuality, of autonomy, from the collective persona of the married individual. An interviewee told me that, for her, keeping secret from her husband the existence of her lover had given her a sense of space, a haven from the subsumation of the marriage, where she could explore her own sexuality, dream her dreams, and enjoy total control over a part of herself. She said, 'Every woman needs something that is hers alone. Some of my friends have their kitties, some their afternoon poker games. I have Sunil.'

It is about more than being just a wife or a husband, a mother or a father, a homemaker or a breadwinner, it is about the need for that 'I', even if for a few fleeting moments.

I have documented during my research quite a few instances where the affair is not at all about the other partner in marriage. Some asserted they were in fact quite happy with their spouses, but just felt a strong need to experience others, to regain the 'I' from the overwhelming 'we'.

Last resort?

Affairs can be the last nail on the coffin for a relationship truly *not* meant to work. Some use their escapades as an excuse to leave a spouse. The sustained feeling of completeness with an affair partner—emotionally, sexually, intellectually, etc.—can mean that something fundamental that they value immensely is missing in their primary bond.

The mind-body affair that has passed its otherwise natural timeline of two to three years can be genuinely threatening to a marriage because it feels so 'right.' This may be particularly hurtful if the abandoned marital partner is genuinely involved in his/her spouse and the other has moved away and not just in a temporary sense. It is then that the affair is truly tragic for both but perhaps far more hurtful for the one being abandoned than the one who has found the connection with another.

Think about it...

Here's a thought, for the one disowned: If you are not getting the love, how does it matter if someone else gets it? Also, in the end, if your partner develops that bond with that someone else, can you really control it? Can you influence it in any way? Most importantly, should you?

Conclusion

Everyone's monogamy agreement is different. Emotions associated with a committed relationship are seldom cut and dried. No one can really tell you what to do or what it means in your relationship to be monogamous. You have to decide what is important. Instead of playing the perpetrator and the victim card, perhaps the two can sit and deconstruct the affair and see where the two marriage partners really are.

An affair is not about integrity. People are ambivalent. It is never black and white. To assign a singular meaning to an affair is oversimplification. Like Esther Perel, the author of *Mating in Captivity*, said:

> Though affairs often result in deep emotional crisis, deception and betrayal are not the prime motivation. I suggest we look at infidelity in terms of growth, autonomy, and the desire to reconnect with lost parts of ourselves. Perhaps affairs are also an expression of yearning and loss. Sometimes, we seek the gaze of another not because we reject our partner, but because we are tired of ourselves.'

Yet…

Even if not for the long haul, even when we know that our partner's betrayal is just a temporary dalliance, extramarital relationships paralyze our sense of self, sting us long after the affair partner has left our marital lives and fill us with a sense of dread every time there is a detour in our spouse's schedule or we see them smile while typing in the message box on their cell phones.

Forget a full-fledged affair, even the knowledge that our spouse *may* have been attracted to a certain so-and-so, sends those arsenal-packed bullets piercing right through our hearts. Besides, in our society, the principle reason why a man could not really love a wife who he cheats on, is that his infidelity turns her into a sad victim. She loses her position and self-esteem. Even if the wife was prepared to turn a blind eye to her husband keeping a mistress, her family and friends make sure the drama becomes a crisis.

Jealousy

Jealousy is one such manifestation that shreds our hearts and egos into pieces, Though it has some positive functions, that it can be seen as a sign of commitment and work as a relationship-protection device, and that it plays a welcome part in igniting sexual passion long dead between the couple, it is far more infamous for the destructive experiences that it brings in love relationships recorded in almost all cultures and periods of history.

The ability to synthesize acquired cumulative behaviour and knowledge of our spouse, to read their intentions, to catch in their eyes that slightly lingering glance, the very intimate things that make the couple a couple, can turn into an excruciating curse when one in the couple tries a little uncoupling on the side. Some feel that the only way we can save ourselves the pain is by not *knowing*. Like this lady who wrote to me about her husband, 'He may have his dalliances but god forbid I get a whiff of any of it I will break every bone in his body, and then clean him dry of every rupee he is worth.'

And yet, we cannot help but pursue knowing! Many wrote that they tried not to feel jealous, it was an attempt to save themselves from embarrassment, floundering self-respect, yet the green-eyed monster just rose involuntarily from somewhere within and danced its famous tandav.

Detective agencies thrive in urban India. We may have the satisfaction of our suspicions proving correct, but once we know those details, we cannot 'un-know' them. They will burn us afresh with every recall! A friend who discovered her husband's affair from a hotel bill has not been able to bring herself to go to the hotel even for a meal, even though four years have passed since her discovery.

Jealousy sears us enough to push some of us into criminal behaviour. Everyday, newspapers report crimes of passion, acid throwing, murders, abandonment, etc.

The sexual leads to the emotional!

Chances are that sexual intimacy with the lover will lead to emotional closeness over time and this can be seriously threatening to the marriage, for it can cause dents in the strictly 'not-to-be-touched' emotional exclusivity clause—which in some cases is the only comforting exclusive feature that has remained once the romance and passion has faded. Also, emotional exclusivity and its accompanying security is the pot of gold for which a lot of nonsense is tolerated by both parties within a marriage.

The thrill-seekers, here too, may think that they can uncouple the sexual from the emotional and keep it compartmentalized. Yet, in many cases people find themselves getting more attached to their affair partners than they had bargained for, which ultimately starts affecting the emotional quotient in their marriage too! The book *Intimacies* by William Jankowiak states,

'Clearly passionate love and sex are separate domains. What is striking, however, is how easily they merge into one another.'

No wonder long-term extramarital affairs begin to resemble their own marriages after a point! A classical instance is the character of Emma Bovary in Gustav Flaubert's *Madame Bovary*, who discovers in her illicit affairs all the banality of marriage.

What when the fields start overlapping?

Remember the joke, 'I have everything; romance, passion, companionship and money, of course I have to make sure the men do not bump into each other!'

We seek from an extramarital relationship what we miss in our marriage, be it romance or passion, the need for attention or praise, to be wild and kinky or all of them together. In a sense we bring two very different selves to two widely divergent relationships. In one we may be mature, rational, practical and realistic (what normally comes with marriage) while in the other we may don our 'naughty' hats, be carefree, wild, dreamy and unreal; essentially everything that comes with the extramarital turf! It may very well be that the two selves are like two different people, almost like a split personality. In our minds we can justify that we are in essence fulfilling from one, what, in any case, is not in the other. Though we may still feel some amount of guilt, yet this theorization affords us some sense of manageability. In our minds we are convinced that the two are separate domains and can coexist with some dexterity here, some secrecy there. Besides, the romance in the extramarital can bring back the zing in the primary relationship too. The desire in one can rekindle the passion in the other.

But what if the attraction develops into something deeper? What when the different selves and their roles start merging? What when the romance bond starts getting into the 'caring' one? What when the light starts getting heavy? Can we then manage ourselves with the blurring boundaries? What when one starts demanding more than the other is ready to give?

There can then be confusion, acute psychological anxiety, and all three must but suffer. This is the phase when either our guilt eats us up or the unmanageability of it gives us away. The moving of passionate love towards a more companionate one in an affair, creates havoc with our primary marital bond and the very real and solid love, self -destroying our sense of control and, with it, our lives!

And for the rare few who do find true love in an affair—they have all the guilt and the hurt and the mess to deal with. Can one girl's heart be worth another girl's hurt?

For some it is, and yet, I cannot help but remember this line from the movie *Last Night*, 'It's the years you can't undo. You will never be able to take away the years with her husband. And the moment you try, this will be gone.'

So are we doomed if we do and doomed if we don't?

Dr Kushal Jain of VIMHANS related an interesting incident to me. A 35-year-old housewife, married to a rich businessman, came to see him with a man. She began by telling him of her great anxiety. The man with her said she suspected him of having an affair. Sensing something untoward, Dr Jain asked the man who he really was. Both showed acute discomfort; the woman finally told him the man with her was her boyfriend.

Dr Jain, 'What to do? I am not only dealing with counselling husband and wife, I am dealing with counselling of extramarital relationships. Then I spoke to her and understood that husband is not available. She has a kid. I asked the woman what her expectations are from her husband. She said, 'He needs to love me, take care of me, not to do anything with anyone except with me." Then I asked her, "What are your expectations from your boyfriend?" She said, "I have no such expectations from my boyfriend—he can do whatever he wants—it's an okay thing." I asked her why she wasn't leaving her husband. Her reply was, "My husband is a rich man and so with him I have a better future. But I'm not happy, so I am having this affair." She added, "My boyfriend is not loyal to me."

'I said, "No, the problem does not lie with your boyfriend—the problem in a way lies within you. You are giving the liberty of a husband to your boyfriend, but what you are expecting from your boyfriend is akin to that of a husband. Mentally, the boyfriend is acting like a husband—except being the provider. If you pull your boyfriend too close and treat him like a husband, the boyfriend also starts acting like a husband. He would want that you leave everything and go to him. Will you be able to do that?" Then I told her that the basic issue is to clear the boundaries. "You have to accept the fact that boyfriend is a boyfriend—he will stray. Because if you have one leg inside and one leg outside, the boyfriend will also have one leg inside and one leg outside the relationship."'

In spite of hopeful claims and positive assertions, many researchers have shown that concurrent love is inherently fragile, unstable, and seldom long-lasting. We suspect that, while there may be occasionally successful concurrent love relationships, ethnographic and historical studies repeatedly document it is not feasible on a larger community scale.

As William Jankowiak rightly said, in his work *Intimacies*:

> No culture is ever completely successful or satisfied, with its synthesis or reconciliation of passionate companion (or comforts) love and sexual desire. Whether in a technological metropolis or in a simple farming community, a tension exists between sexual mores and proscriptions governing the proper context for love... But what human communities have in common is a universal compulsion to make a working peace with the three-way conflict of romance/passionate love, comfort/attachment love, and physical sex.

The emotional tug between the competing and often contradictory desires ensures that every generation will revisit, renegotiate, and modify its 'traditions' that account for the relationship between love and sex.

Points to ponder

Researchers note that infidelities have increased even when divorce has become available, accepted, and largely non-stigmatized. Infidelity is a worldwide phenomenon that occurs with remarkable regularity, despite near-universal disapproval of this behaviour.

What if we stopped describing infidelity in terms of perpetrators and victims, damages and costs? For when we do so, we focus on the trauma of it rather than trying to understand the difficulty in reconciling attachment and desire with the same person.

What if we have not accepted the possibility of complexity and ambivalence in our highly developed brain systems? Accept that knowing what we want in the realm of love and intimacy isn't an exact science! That lying in an intimate relationship may simply mean that our emotions have not fallen in step with institutional diktats—the easy but facile arrangement between the forces of passionate love, comfort love, and sexual desire. What if the arrangement is not as ideologically and structurally sound as we have been told it is?

What if we see that there are worse ways people cheat on each other? From being indifferent to cruel while staying faithful! From neglecting the needs to not respect the spouse while sleeping and waking up next to them everyday. From cavernous, empty silences to lying about any and every thing even as they hold joint bank accounts. Even the most solidly united couples lead double or triple lives, especially when they both work, and adultery is only one of the countless ways of being elsewhere.

What if those who are monogamous try and understand why being monogamous is so much harder than they've been led to believe? What if your truth is not your spouse's truth?

Think about it...

There's an entire industry with a serious financial stake in upholding the idea that cheating is desperately serious, a symptom of a deeply flawed marriage, of two people who need to be cured. We are being flooded with images of sex—whether it is in advertisements of chocolates, jewellery, house paint or a deodorant—tied up with sexuality. Besides, if we look at the latest trend in advertising, the ads make you appear 'cooler' via portraying infidelity, even promiscuity.

What if, even if acceptance is difficult, we can at least try to understand this desire for passion; and thus, escape from the maudlin unhappiness which stands pitted against our hankering for stability.

What if passion did not equal love, and the loss of one did not necessarily mean the loss of the other? What if we look at fidelity as a commitment to the working partnership and not to one another? What of the importance of shared history, things accomplished together, like a home, kids, life challenges—financial, health, social, etc. that have been dealt with and overcome—and then one has an affair and all the years in between become false or failed?

Why do we feel the need to cloak relationships under love? What if we stop using *love* for lust, desire, infatuation, or simple 'adding spice to life'? Things would be far less complicated, wouldn't it?

When we divorce love from the concept of ownership, what happens?

What if marriages are ruined by monogamy?

Like Alexander Dumas said, 'The bonds of wedlock are so heavy that it takes two to carry them, sometimes three.'

The chaotic richness of life...

For some of us, monogamy is essential for the relationship to feel safe and stable. Yet our beliefs may change as we age or our situations change. There are others who may experiment with other mating strategies and find their own level suited to the loved ones involved. We are complex creatures and there is no one 'right' or 'wrong' way. The way we choose to love is no one else's business but those involved in it. Yet, we as a society feel compelled to pass judgement about the sexual behaviour of others, more often than not even without attempting to know the complex and varied forces behind it. And really, even if we try, can we really understand the dynamics of a relationship that we are not a part of?

Relationships are tricky anyway without us outsiders layering it with our half-baked knowledge and sketchy awareness. In his book, *Invented Moralities: Sexual Ethics in an Age of Uncertainty*, British sociologist Jeffrey Weeks asks if it's possible to find democratic principles for judging each other's drives, desires and decisions. He believes so—provided we begin 'rethinking values by exploring in a positive manner the sexual and moral diversity that causes so much dread...'

5

We Are Like That Only!

The fact is, we are much more afraid of life than our ancestors, and cannot find it in our hearts either to marry or not to marry. Marriage is terrifying, but so is a cold and forlorn old age.

—ROBERT LOUIS STEVENSON

We live in a very different world today. The old hierarchies of protection and dependency no longer exist. Traditions, old mores and loyalties, are loosening their hold. Old models and structures stand today in deep conflict with our new systems and way of living. And yet, our basic human need for companionship and love is as intact as ever. If at all, it is even more acute today, simply because the inner circle of our loved ones has shrunk so drastically. And yet, we still want witnesses to our lives and still wish to be witnesses to theirs. The more we gain in awareness and freedom, in equality and individuality, the more lonely—and emotionally dependent—

we are. Imbalanced and un-whole, we still want it all, to *be* and to matter to another.

There are two sides to the differences of yore and now—the actual state of affairs, and, our awareness of and attitudes towards it. Not only has the DNA of how we perceive love relationships undergone a massive change, there is also a huge amplification in the impact of its awareness in our everyday lives. Each provides further momentum to the other, posing us challenges of unprecedented complexity. We are not only aware but feel obliged to act on our awareness. And this inevitably slips us right back into the fundamental inconsistencies between two individuals locked in a love unit. For, in the end, all couples today are two *aware* beings, not only dealing with their own ambitions and inconsistencies while trying to chalk out a shared life together, but also facing their partners' ambitions often at loggerheads with their own, and their partners' own inconsistencies. It is akin to walking on the razor's edge. There is always opportunity cost, no matter how heavy or light we tread, no matter on which side we lean more, no matter what rational or irrational arguments we employ to convince ourselves of our then dispositions. Our essential needs will always be at loggerheads with that of our significant fundamental others.

The paradox that we are

> For wanting to belong to one, but congenitally tempted by others
> For demanding space one moment, and aching to merge the next

For feeling safe in familiarity, but thirsting for novelty
For demanding the right to explore, and *be* but anxious to *home* as soon as the terror of distance dawns;
For the impulse to share all, and be bored because we *know* all;
For wanting to be transparent, but also needing privacy;
For asking for freedom, but not willing to reciprocate;
For desiring immortality (through a legacy, a child), but also wanting to live life unfettered;
For exploiting the vulnerabilities of our loved ones, because we know we can;
For hurting the person we love, even while knowing we should forgo and forget;
For knowing that loving more means less power, and more power means *I love less*—yet not accepting one and not understanding the other;
For demanding unconditional acceptance, but holding the loved one accountable for every little folly.

No wonder the chaos! But what can be done? What are our alternatives?

Perhaps it is time for us to open our minds and think, really think, about relationships. We must ruminate and enquire, debate and discuss, pose our issues and look for solutions. We must express and communicate, and we must encourage our significant other(s) to do the same. And we must seek help from professionals if we feel the need.

And perhaps in the reading and the talking, in the listening and the thinking, we might be able to revisit and renegotiate. And, most importantly, understand our own selves and those we hold dearer than our very lives.

Perhaps we need to accept that:

Even as I *know* my partner in some profound sense, in many ways I don't.

That my freedom plus my partner's freedom is not a utopian path to love.

My—or my partner's—infidelity may not be the last, simply the next.

I cannot love—or *unlove*—at will.

Old desires will wither with age, but also rekindle with time.

That even as it is a difficult journey, it is worth sharing.

That I—or my partner—will love as much and as well, as humans can—that is, imperfectly.

Acknowledgements

To my mom and dad, for I saw them stand beside each other through the thick and thin; it has been more than 50 years!

To Sanjeev, who did not flinch or tell me off even when he had to go through in our relationship whatever I was reading and researching about other couples!

To my sisters, Suman and Priti for all the humour they made me see that marriage forces you to!

To my little girls, Aishwarya and Sanaya, who had to grow up faster than normal as we discussed theories and experiences!

To Manjushree, thanks for those long discussions on love and relationship.

To Rajat, for helping me edit and structure it.

Thanks, I will always be indebted.